C000285538

Gary's daily dose of positiv
taking another vitamin eac
vitamin C & cod liver oil
weather, no matter what's going on in this crazy
world, matter what the news in the media each day,
Gary's Don't Be A Goose daily boost is a sure way to
pull ANYONE up by the bootstraps, ensuring we all
focus on the positive & I for one, am eternally
grateful for his constant reminders that attitudes are
totally contagious - so I'm making sure mine is worth
catching each day, thanks to Gazza Bounce Time!
Marie Cross

When scrolling down Facebook and YouTube, I
always enjoy seeing my Gazza Bounce Time video
and look forward to getting my daily dose of positive
attitude!
Positivity is massively important but not always easy,
so it's great to receive these messages, so I'm on
course for the day!
The messages are always well thought out,
motivating, inspiring and on the money, so it's now
become a key part of my day!
I just need to keep this positive attitude and always
avoid being that goose!
Thanks
Richard Rumbelow

Gary, firstly I wanted to say you're amazing and
thank you for being my friend. You are an
inspiration. Your daily dose of positive attitude
makes my heart smile. When I'm having a tough and
challenging day I know, I can take a look at one of

your posts and it puts the bounce back in my step and reminds me that anything is possible.
Laura Moxham

Gary, you are a true inspiration.
You've been through some tough times in your business, as have I. I think that's why I connected with you at the start. We had something in common, and I really admired how you handled it and how you turned your attitude around.
Your daily videos are a great reminder to me that life is good, makes me thankful for my wonderful wife and daughters, my health and happiness. It also helps keep me focused on doing the things that move the needle and not be distracted.
I love your attitude.
Your kindness and generosity shine. You're a wonderful human being, and I honestly wish you all the happiness and good that life can bring.
What have I changed?
My attitude and outlook.
I'm no longer concerned about what others have, what my competition does, what anyone thinks. I will do what's right for me and my family.
Do good for others.
See the good in any situation and speak well of my competition.
No time for negative people in my life anymore.
Big love brother.
Adrian McGivern

DON'T BE A GOOSE

Let your passion set you free

Gary Fullwood

3P PUBLISHING

To
Christine -
Be Brave, Be Beautiful
Be Awesome

Love
Gary

First published in 2016 in the UK

3P Publishing
C E C, London Road
Corby
NN17 5EU

A catalogue number for this book is available from
the British Library

ISBN 978-1-911559-14-6

Cover design: Jamie Rae

Don't Be A Goose

My mum, my dad, my wife, Linda, my four boys and all the friends that supported me through the good and bad times.

Nigel Botterill for inspiring the EC Family and me for always believing.

Andy Gibney and 3P Publishing for making this possible.

And, to my superstar and hero, Ossie Robinson, for showing me the 'never give up' attitude.

The bravest boy I know.

Gary

Contents

Foreword

Gary Fullwood is a freak of nature. It's been my pleasure to know him for the last five years during which time I've witnessed at close quarters the extraordinary ups and downs of his life.

He first came to my attention when he turned up at one of our big Entrepreneurs Circle events in the North West dressed in tight denim shorts - and little else! The topless Mr Fullwood, waxed to within an inch of his life, made sure that every other business owner there that day (and there were over 600 of them) knew who he was.

But Gary's not a show-off. Not really.

When he sits around the Mastermind table, we see the 'real' Gary. The Gary in this book. He's searingly honest.

Vulnerable.
Authentic.
And fun.

On some occasions, Gary is like a little lost boy. Other times he's rampant. Like a lion.

What he's achieved with Watford Bathrooms and Kitchens is a story worth telling. And one worth paying attention to for any aspiring entrepreneur. It's Gary's story. And it's full of oversights, mistakes, cock-ups and missed opportunities. And failure too. But there's also remarkable achievements. Big gigantic bounce-backs. Huge leaps. Bravado. And success.

Our hero doesn't hold back. He shares it all - and it ain't all pretty. But it's real. And it's human. And it's Gary. Gary, the man who has enriched more lives than he'll ever realise. Gary the man who brings more smiles to more rooms than anyone else I know.

Gary the ball of energy. Gary, a man so completely unemployable he HAD to make his business a success.

A lot of very dull business people have written a lot of very dull business books. But this isn't one of them.

So well done for holding a copy of Gary's book. What you have in your hands is a literary rollercoaster. It will make you feel a bit sick at times. You might even cry. But there'll be adrenaline and highs, and when you've finished it, you'll be glad you took the ride. And then, in his own small way, Gary will have enriched your life too.

Because he's a force of nature...not a freak. Oh, and don't worry, he hasn't died. That wasn't a eulogy you've just read. And I strongly suspect that this is only Volume One because the best is yet to come...

Enjoy

Nigel Botterill
November 2016

Chapter One

Waking up with a positive attitude

It's time to wake up, not just today or tomorrow, but for the rest of my life. I have learnt that the only way to wake up in the mornings is with a positive attitude. This is so important to how any of my days begin because "you are what you think about, all day every day." This saying has changed the course of my life along with so many other mind-sets and mind shifts, but today I'm talking about how you bounce yourself out of bed every morning and being so excited, knowing today is going to be a better day than yesterday, just by opening my eyes.

Anyone who knows me, knows I'm quite an excitable bouncy person anyway, but it has not always been that way, especially on the inside, even though the outside shows and tells a different story. I have had to learn what my passions are and what gets me excited. For the last three years, I have suffered breakdowns in my life where I have fallen so hard and crumbled. I have had to lock myself in a room and block the whole world out, all because I had no structure to my amazing positive attitude. I could not believe it myself, but, yes you need 100% structure for your attitude to work and to make shit happen.

You see I was like most normal average people, and on Christmas Day I would think about what I am going to change about myself on January 1st and create my New Year's resolution. On that day I would go hell for leather in trying to prove to myself I can do this, and for a couple of months I would be flying, nothing could stop me! Then all of a sudden I would feel myself start to deteriorate and slow down because I would lose focus and get bored. A lot of this came down to who I was surrounding myself with as well as what I was watching and reading. This all seems to happen in the subconscious mind, and this has been one of my massive learnings from life. I did not take advantage enough of the other truly remarkable people I could call upon in my time of need. Let's get one thing straight; I'm not for one second knocking any of my friends that I have surrounded myself with because that has been a massive part of my journey and has helped me learn how to create myself. However, because of the world we live in is such a negative one, we get suckered into negative actions that are not even our own. This is where I had to be strong and get over it by realising what I wanted, not what others wanted from me. This was my problem, I was not strong enough and slowly "The Drains" would suck the life out of me and I could not be bothered to get up in the mornings. This is where the plodding along begins and the "just doing enough and get by in life" starts to happen.

Now when I'm bouncing off the walls in the mornings, something is seriously wrong because to some people I'm that annoying, stupidly happy person, who just cannot stop smiling, singing and dancing about itching to get on with my day. If you ask my wife, she gets a neck ache in the mornings just trying to talk to me because I cannot keep still. So this is why you have to have structure on how you wake up in the mornings; it's imperative that this happens and, most importantly, the structure has to become a habit, maybe even more important than brushing your teeth. (But please keep brushing your teeth, at least twice a day.)

So, after a very shit second half of the year in 2014, on December 20th I made a stance, some may even say I had an epiphany, and it was time to create my own habit of how I can start every day with the biggest bounce that I had ever achieved. I told myself I'm going to be positive no matter what, no one is going to put me down anymore as I know there is greatness inside of me dying to get out and be shared with the world. It's "Gazza Bounce Time".

I started to think about all the great books I have read and all the great audios I have listened to over the years and how I could use that information to my advantage; before long I was on my iPad researching these great legends and seriously putting my life into perspective.

I mean all the crazy shit that goes on in the world and all the people that are in such bad places, how the hell can I complain or moan about my day? I mean, Gary sort your life out bruver...

This is where it all falls into place; it's just so damn easy to find positive information and vibes nowadays especially with the internet, YouTube, audible, podcasts and Kindle, the list just goes on and on its endless and you just need to embrace it.

So, first things first I created a Pinterest wall and called it my "positive attitude board." I searched and searched for positive quotes to add to my board, I was already smiling so hard just from reading these, as they make so much sense when you take them in. I then started searching YouTube for positive and motivational videos to watch. I would add these to my favourites and make sure I could watch them over and over again. Next, it was onto my Kindle to download some more amazing books to read and listen to on audible. So, here I am with all this information at my disposal, now what do I do with it? This was where I had to truly commit to a positive attitude, that's right, no messing about as I have now made that decision to wake up for the rest of my life and start making shit happen. It was time to start bouncing out of my bed ready for my day, every day, for the rest of my life.

I start my day at 5am every single day, yes that's right, 5am every morning, YES.

I have set my alarm to go off at 5am to the sound of *My Boulder* by the *King Blues*. This is a tune that just for some reason holds a meaning to me, so along with the words and the beat itself, it gets me ready to bounce.

Friends have always been a massive part of my life, so the feeling knowing that they are there for me and I will always be there for them, is what starts my engine for my positive attitude.

The second step in my day is my little outburst of self-affirmation in the mirror, so with a jump, a growl and a silly face, this confirms I am up and ready for my day along with the realisation that yes, I am a little strange!

The next step is a Pinterest quote, searching out a quote that truly inspires me and gets me thinking right for the day, this will then get pinned and saved to my camera roll on my phone. The reason for this is so that I can share that positive attitude and thought with the rest of the world on Facebook and Instagram. It really helps me knowing that everybody else knows what mood I am in and how positive I'm feeling, so hopefully, a little bit of bounce kicks them up the arse too.

Now for the next step. I am straight onto YouTube to begin my search for inspirational videos and icons to listen to. The sound of their powerful voices while I'm in the shower just goes right through my body as I repeat their words of wisdom over and over again like a man possessed.

Then, when I'm dressed, I look at my own "Power Quote" which says, "You take on the responsibility for making your own dreams a reality." Make sure you have your own power quote or just get one from the internet and look at it every day. I also recommend reading it out loud; this helps the words to resonate within your soul.

Now it's time to get in my car and continue listening to one of my inspirational YouTube videos, but at a very high volume. I'm all alone in my car, while shouting out the words. (You should see the looks I get when I'm at the lights, and they are red.) I arrive at work around 6am and I'm truly at my bounciest now and ready to start my ninety minutes (this is something we will get to later on). Nothing can stop my positive attitude because the only intake I have had since the minute I opened my eyes at 5am is pure happiness, inspiration, motivation and positivity.

This is now the only habit I believe in, this is my morning life, and I swear by it. This is why while I am writing this I have the biggest smile on my face like you would not believe. Life is just awesome because it is what you make of it that makes the difference. A positive attitude is totally infectious, and that is why, me Gary Fullwood, a bathroom designer from Watford needs to share how you can change your life just by tweaking and altering a few negative bad habits into super amazing positive attitude thoughts. So join me today and start bouncing everywhere you go, from the second you open your eyes.

The Gazza Bounce structure and formula to waking up every morning with a ridiculously amazing, positive attitude.

- Set your alarm ringtone/sound to something that motivates and inspires you.
- Jump out of bed smiling knowing that a new day can only mean new possibilities.
- Look in that mirror, pull a silly face, shake your head, growl (Grrrrrr) and say, "Don't be a goose, I'm awesome and today is going to be amazing."
- Pick out your quote of the day from Pinterest, read it and truly believe it.

- Get your YouTube motivational video ready to play. If you do not know any inspirational icons, just type in motivational video and select anything that comes up. I can promise you it will get you pumped and ready for your day and you will find someone you relate to and enjoy their tone of voice.
- Make sure you do not have any crap radio stations on in your car that has news on it!! This is totally unacceptable, and I FORBID it. Only motivational sounds allowed turned up to the max. Please make sure you are shouting and repeating what they are saying.
- Have written somewhere in clear view your "Power Quote." This is your positive attitude message, which you must read every single day before leaving your house.
- Arrive at work, bounce out of your car smiling as you walk into work. This creates that infectious positive attitude feeling, setting the example that today is going to be an amazing day.

That is my daily positive attitude structure to waking up every single day in the right frame of mind and ready for the day ahead. You have to repeat this and make it a habit. You also need to tweak this, so it suits you and by doing this over and over again watch how your life changes for the better.

A positive attitude, the only way to wake up.

Chapter Two

Emotional drivers

One of the most powerful reasons for my true determination and drive comes down to emotional drivers. To succeed in life and, achieve greatness, you need to have goals and dreams, but even having them is not enough, you need to have a reason to want to reach them, and this is what I call an emotional driver.

An emotional driver is something that is deep within you; this is something that eats at you and tells you why succeeding means so much. Everyone has their own and sometimes people don't even realise them at first, but they are there, and they are hungry. This is the time to discover why you want to be better than who you are now. To help you with this, I will first of all share mine.

There are a number of different reasons as to why people push themselves so hard in life and each individual will have a different type of driver. They are generally caused by our own experiences in life, not always traumatic; sometimes it's just the environment we are brought up in and live in. It is so important that we understand our emotional drivers because it becomes our power tool and gives us the ability to influence the habits and structure we require to succeed.

There are so many different types of emotional drivers, and it's not always one that inspires us. Here are a few that will give you an idea and sense of what I'm talking about:

- Belonging/Love – Feel part of something
- Security – Feeling safe and secure
- Diversity – Having a variety of more
- Recognition – Gaining awards and stature
- Achievement – Self-satisfaction and pride
- Contribution – The need to give back

There are many more, and to some people, they all have different meanings.

My emotional drivers stem right back to childhood and are a mixture of a few of the above.

My first emotional driver would have to be belonging/love as my dad was not about a lot during my childhood and my mum had to struggle in life; working as many jobs as she could juggle, so that me, my brother and two sisters never went without. It is not until you grow up that you understand the hardship our parents go through to make sure we are all happy.

This is where my first driver comes into play because I have four kids of my own now, two stepsons and two boys of my own. My ultimate aim is to make sure they never go through what I did when I was young.

This is not a matter of just giving them what they want; the ultimate point is just being a dad and making sure I'm there for them in their time of need. There are always going to be rough times, and we certainly have had a fair few of them, but because of my emotional driver I am more determined to push past any obstacles that are put in my way, and that has helped me no end.

My boys are my life, and I will never give up on them no matter what, but to achieve this, I have had to stay positive and keep my beliefs strong. Could it be that my dad not being around was really a good thing, as it has led to this desire to provide for my family? Who knows? Except that it has left me with this overwhelming feeling of family love.

I just want to make one thing clear at this stage, I love my dad to bits. He has had many other strengths in different areas as I grew up, but there is no denying my younger experiences have made this driver crucial to who I am now and how I think about certain aspects of my life.

I have known so many people who blame their parents for who they are and why they are the person they are when life is shit for them, but I'm sorry this is just a lame excuse for making the wrong choices in your life. You don't have to sit around feeling sorry for yourself and using excuses for being lazy; you are the only person in the world who can tell you what path is right or wrong.

My second emotional driver will have a mixture of recognition and achievement; this is because of how crap I found school life.

I was so excited to start senior school, and I made a very bold decision when I was in junior school, I decided I wanted to go to a different school to all my friends because I wanted to change and stop being influenced. Being honest I was a little ratbag, but only because I could not sit still and had a very short attention span. Obviously, I was too bouncy.

However, I soon got a big bump and my first real knock back in life. This came about on my first P.E lesson; I was so excited it was P.E as I loved sport. It is the one thing I know I'm really good at and have loads of energy to participate in. As I'm getting changed into my kit, I pull out my fresh new trainers and the taunting and laughing begins. Virtually the whole class is pointing and laughing at me; my trainers cost about £3 from Bovingdon Market and everyone else was wearing all the branded names, Nike, Adidas, Puma and it hurt like hell. I was tarred as the pikey kid, just because I didn't have designer trainers. Bloody kids can be so horrible.

The second experience came on the first non-uniform day, and from the previous story you can probably already see where this is going, you would have thought I would have learnt. I still thought it was cool that I didn't have to wear a school uniform and I was really looking forward to this. I put my favourite t-shirt on, a pair of jogging bottoms and my trainers. Wow! What an experience that was, the laughing didn't stop from the minute I got to school. I was so hurt by this, and it scared me for a long time. That day I left school, and it was so embarrassing that I made sure every time one of those days came up I was always ill. I couldn't ever compete with the designer clothes that everyone else wore, so I never risked it. From these two stories, you will now understand that my image is one of the most important things to me now. The difference is that I now have my own image, my own style and I don't care what people think as I won't be judged. I am who I am, and if people don't like what they see, it doesn't matter because it is absolutely none of their business.

The next experience from senior school was with the football team, our first football P.E lesson. Like most kids, I loved football and could not wait for this one. I had a fire in my belly and just wanted to get cracking and play, but the teachers had other ideas. How the teachers went about this, still disgusts me to this day! We all got told to sit down on the field and then they asked: "Those of you, who play for a football team outside of school, put your hands up."

Mine did not go up.

"Right," they continued, "You lot go over there, and the rest of you stay here."

From that day forward, for four years, they were the school football team, and the teachers didn't give anyone else a chance, no one even got a look in. They didn't know if any of us were any good and they didn't care. Obviously, there were a few kids that weren't remotely bothered by this and, in their own way relieved, but my heart was broken. It was yet another painful experience I had to take away from school.

I was at that school for four years, and I played one game for the school; this was not because of my ability, this was because most of the players took a stand and refused to play unless I got the chance. Every week I would walk past that selection board just hoping that I might for once see my name up there, but it never happened. I suppose this is life and, as we all know it is here to test us, so sod them.

All it did was make me stronger and more determined to be a footballer and prove I was good enough, and that is exactly what I did.

Outside of school, I made it my mission to prove how good I was. I played district football, county football and when I left school I even had trials for some professional football clubs. I also played at a very high standard on Saturdays and Sundays, playing semi-professional football for a little while getting £50 a game. Whoop whoop!

I succeeded because I wasn't going to let someone tell me I'm not good enough without giving me a chance. You can knock me as much as you want, but all I will do is take it as a positive to push me forward and make me stronger and better. It makes you think then, was this a great experience? I have to say yes because it put me in good stead for a happy career in football as I achieved so many targets and won so many trophies.

I know it sounds like school was my worst nightmare, but I have my last painful experience to share and another truly beneficial driver to add to my growing success as a business owner. This one comes from the teachers in general, as they had no faith in me academically. I'm not going to hide the fact I was not the easiest pupil, but does that mean you should give up on kids? I may have a short attention span, but surely the right buttons are not being hit to satisfy what could have helped so many other kids who fail and me? It became a normal day at school for me being told I was a waste of time and a waste of space. Always being told I had no future, I will be a failure and my life will amount to nothing. What gives teachers the right to judge a kid and tell them that?

Let's get some perspective, my grammar may not be the best, I'm sure there are plenty of spelling mistakes, and I'm not the best at maths. But, I own my own business, and I'm the one sitting here writing my first book with the biggest smile on my face. The thing they didn't account for was my ambition, my desire and my determination to be a better me. They didn't want to give me an opportunity because I didn't sit still in class, but that's why I created my opportunities in life. Some people will say that maybe it was a good thing they were so horrible and couldn't be bothered, but the fact is I have worked so bloody hard to be in this position. I have read the right books, I have studied the right type of information, and I have sat through seminars and been on courses, all to enhance my self development. I have also made sure I surrounded myself with the right people in order to make something of myself and create my own better future.

No one will ever dictate my direction in life because all decisions will be my own.

For some of you reading this, you will see my school life and experiences as a disaster. Not getting on with teachers, being laughed at and finally being expelled. But the real fact is, it probably was the best life lesson I could ever have had. I learned that kids are just kids and some of them are mature adults now and greater friends. I also learnt that school didn't stimulate the part of the brain that needed stimulating. School was not right for me, but most importantly it was the ultimate driver for my true success. That is being the man I am today, the passion, the desire and the emotion that comes out of me is because I never go into anything half-heartedly, everything I do, I commit to with every part of my heart.

My last emotional driver is "Contribution", and this is what I'm doing now. I'm sharing my story in the hope it will inspire others to truly believe in themselves and to do something with their lives. I get so much satisfaction from sharing my big learns in life, and it is one of my dreams to help inspire thousands of people into achieving their own goals and dreams like I am.

I make motivational videos, and I bounce around telling everyone how amazing they are, just so they feel good about themselves. Happiness is infectious along with smiling. Start doing it more and do what makes you happy. I will always support great charities and causes, and the more I push myself to get closer to my dreams, I know I will have the power to make a bigger difference in the world. As long as I am making a difference in one person's life, that is all that matters.

I hope you understand my drivers and why they are so important for what the future holds for you. It's time for you to discover your emotional drivers and be who you want to be and stop letting someone else dictate who you should be. Look deep into yourself, start writing things down, and you will discover your purpose. It's time to start creating yourself and the best time to do that is now.

Chapter Three

Inspirational people

All through our lives, there are many people that influence us and our actions. It all starts at a young age, as we get inspired by all sorts of TV programmes, movies and sports. It is the superstars that are on TV give us that motivation to be someone else, to be someone superhuman and awesome.

My first vivid memory and the first influence on my life would have to be Sylvester Stallone from the first *Rocky* movie. What an amazing movie; this was someone who had nothing going for him, but when it came to passion, desire and pure determination, Rocky had it in abundance. I was so inspired, so motivated and all that just from a film.

I used to re-enact all the great scenes from that movie as a kid in my living room. I would drive my mum absolutely bonkers: cushions being punched, running up my stairs at the end of my training, just like Rocky did when he accelerated away from all the kids chasing him (yes, I love that scene). I even used to do the "Yo Adrian, I did it," part and let's not forget the E*ye of the Tiger* song that still gets me pumped no matter when I hear it. You want to put it on, don't you?

Don't Be A Goose

I know I am reminiscing now but please bear with me. As children, we are influenced by so much, and for the last couple of years, I have paid more and more attention to these characters and what they have achieved in life. Sylvester Stallone is a genius of a man, and the words he puts into his movies are inspirational in themselves. I never became a boxer, although my mum forced me to go, and I wasn't bad as a youngster, but it wasn't my calling.

Another inspiration for me was the legend that is Ryan Giggs; almost from the minute he burst onto the scene at Manchester United in 1991 as an 18-year-old boy. He is my footballing hero, and I'm still disappointed and gutted that I have still not had the opportunity to meet him and shake his hand personally. There's plenty of time though, and it's on my goal wall. We are talking about a man that has been there and done it all in football, played at the highest level, for, what I consider, the greatest club in the world, year after year. You cannot do that without having a vision, dreams, goals, 100% commitment and surrounding yourself with influential people. Alex Ferguson is another book altogether. So many youngsters get that chance and cannot stay focused to see it through; that is why as I have got older, I have respected him more and more and put him on a pedestal for setting an example and being inspirational to so many kids, and adults, in and out of football.

When you grow up, and you are trying to find your way in life it is so crucial that you learn from people who are further along the path than you and can offer that inspiration and guidance. So many have achieved what you want to achieve, and they are willing to share their story if you are confident enough just to ask.

From a very early age, I had to work, and I got taken under the wing of my old boss John Okell at a company called Watford Bathrooms. To start with he was just my boss making me do all the crap jobs in the back of the warehouse, and for me, at the time it was just a rubbish job, but I always told myself I was destined for better things than just a warehouse boy. John showed his faith in me and because of my past experiences; I had not had a lot of that. I grabbed every opportunity he presented me with to learn as much as I could and more. Sometimes it is not until you look back that you realise what, and how, certain people have influenced you and your chosen path.

Without knowing it, John put me in an excellent position to become a great leader in my field and has helped me to pursue a very good career. Although I am a very determined person, I would like to say a massive thank you to John for being such an influential person in the early days of my chosen career path, as well as aiding me in growing as a person. He saw something in me that many did not, and he gave me a great opportunity to be a part of something when no one else would.

This leads me to friends. I have had so many great friends and associates throughout my life, and no matter whom they are, they have all been a part of my journey and help me craft out the motivated and determined man that I am today. I have always had the attitude that I would do anything for them, and they have given me the same level of support. Every one of them has helped shaped my future in some way or another. Watching my friends grow into great men has had a dramatic effect on how I acted; seeing their success has inspired me to push myself harder to achieve my dreams. I know I am not alone with the experience of great friends and I'm sure many of you will feel the same about your peer group too.

My biggest, and toughest, lesson has come this year when I have had to face the reality of letting go. There comes a time when your journey is travelling in a completely different direction to some of those around you, and you have to start thinking about yourself, your family and your future. This is when you have to make that conscious decision about which friends you need to surround yourself with to help you push forward.

This has improved vastly over the last few years by surrounding myself in a business culture and ultimately getting involved with "The Entrepreneurs Circle." This business learning group gave me access to be surrounded by like-minded people, who are all on the same journey as me. There have been so many people from this group that have been an inspiration to me as well as having a massive influence on the path I am taking. This has been so true this year when I have had to separate myself from some people to make sure my focus has not been damaged, and my mind stays clear. The importance of surrounding yourself with inspirational people is imperative to whether or not you make it in life. Surrounding yourself with people who are more successful than you only enhance your chances of reaching your dreams. It is what keeps that fire in your belly burning and that bounce waiting to spring into action.

The challenging part is when you have to take a long look around you and ask yourself are the people you that you are hanging around with helping you to get you closer to your goals? There is a saying: if you hang around with nine alcoholics, you will become the tenth. If you hang around with nine millionaires, then you will become the tenth. Ask yourself this; who and what do you want to become? I know my path, and I know who I need to surround myself with to achieve my dreams.

This is why I want to say a massive thank you to "The Entrepreneurs Circle," for giving me access to some of the greatest people and friends that I have ever known. Also for sharing the love and inspiration that has influenced me to step out of my comfort zone, which in turn gave me the confidence to write this book.

In this last part, I have to say a massive thank you to the internet, YouTube, books and many other media sources that have made it so easy to get access to the most influential and inspirational minds that have graced our planet. Every time I listen to these greats or read their books, it feels they are in the room with me, and their words sink in as if they are guiding me. The effect these have had on my life, and my journey has been immense; they have enhanced my chances of reaching my goals and dreams, and they continue to do so every day of my life and will do for the rest of it.

This area of learning all began when a good friend presented me with a copy of Jim Rohn's audio discs seven years ago, and I haven't looked back. Jim Rohn is legendary, and my mind has been opened up to every word he said and had to share. My list of authors and speakers is endless and grows by the day.

This is what I mean by surrounding yourself with inspirational and influential people; they don't have to be friends, family or associates. These people can sit in your pocket and be with you every second of every day if needed. They are available at the touch of a button. I can only recommend that you download and watch people who can inspire you and your journey. They have helped me through some bad times, but also the amazing times too because I have created that habit to keep my bounce still as bouncy as ever and will not let that habit get broken.

Open your eyes and your ears and make sure your surroundings only have positivity, encouragement and inspiration; making sure the right influences are being created to fulfil your dreams. It's so important that you follow your heart and listen to your body to keep a life full of bounce so that all the right doors are being chosen for your future.

Below I have made a list of people that I think could help you in your life and with any challenges you might have. I truly hope they impact your life as much as they have mine.

The Gazza Bounce list of Inspirational and Influential People.

- Jim Rohn – The ultimate resource for personal development

- Zig Ziglar – Helping people get everything they want out of life
- Robert Kiyosaki – Financial education
- Napoleon Hill – Amazingly successful author
- Michael E Gerber – Author and business skills
- Jeffery Gitomer – Author and professional speaker
- Brian Tracy – Self-development and time management specialist
- Simon Sinek – leadership expert
- Grant Cardone – Sales and motivational expert
- Mike Michalowicz – Business strategist
- Nigel Botterill – Marketing genius
- Arnold Schwarzenegger – Goal setting inspiration and simply amazing man
- Sylvester Stallone – Influential character
- Michael Jordan – Story of champions
- Les Brown – Genius and motivational speaker
- Vidal Sassoon – Inspirational character

Chapter Four

Affirmations create belief

The idea of repeating affirmations started at a very young age. It is not always about being thick skinned; it's about knowing yourself and knowing what you want to be. To begin with, I didn't have a clue what I wanted to be, but I always knew I was better than what was being said to me. I am always telling my kids, you can be whatever you want to be. It doesn't matter who you are or what your current situation is, you can be whatever, or whoever, you want to be. You have choices in this life, and only you get to make the choices that decide your future. It's down to you to create your destiny, and once you realise this, and truly believe in yourself, then the changes in your life will happen. There is a saying that I tell myself and anyone else who needs some help along the way and it is this. You must sacrifice who you are now to become who you want to be.

I will never say that it is going to be easy to change, but self-affirmations help. They have to become a habit, a positive attitude habit that is drilled into your life but, you also have to nurture the passion, determination and true commitment to follow through.

The repetition of affirmations creates such a strong self-belief that it doesn't matter what people say about you. This is because it is none of your business. I hope I'm making the point clearly. If you keep telling yourself enough how amazing you are and that you can achieve greatness, then things start to come together for real.

All through school I had to tell myself, I am worth something, I will make something of myself; I do have a future (even though I might not know what that was going to be). But without knowing it myself, I was reaffirming that there was greatness inside of me.

It was the same with football at school, the teachers took it upon themselves to decide that I was not good enough to play, but I knew I was and I never let that determine my situation. They could only restrict me so much, but in my own time, and outside of school, I could achieve what I wanted. I was good enough, I could play, and I would be good enough to play to the standard that was expected of me.

When I began my journey into adulthood, I left school with no qualifications and became a labourer for a few builders. The money was good, but I knew it wasn't my calling. My life deserved better than just knocking up muck, so I would tell myself I am more than just a labourer, I wanted more from life. From there I decided I wanted to get into computers. I approached a college and applied for a computer course, but guess what? I got told I wasn't clever enough to be allowed on the course. The crazy thing was my 26-year-old friend who was on the dole applied through the dole office and got accepted and put on a two-year course. It's just laughable what this country does sometimes! I was a sixteen-year-old boy, hungry and determined to make something of my life, and you get told to bugger off as you're too stupid. It's ok though, I believed in myself even if no one else did and I was so determined not to have to eat my words and go back onto that building site.

I finally got myself a job in the back of a bathroom warehouse, not the most glamorous, but it was warmer than the building sites I had worked on. Because of my nature and that I'm an all or nothing sort of guy I became bloody good at it, but again I wanted much more. I would continue to tell myself this over and over again. It doesn't matter what situation you are in; you have the power to better yourself as long as you believe it to be true and you reaffirm it to yourself every single day.

You do need to make sure you have other strong attributes to go alongside this, and by having a passion and determination inside of me along with the emotional drivers, I knew greatness would come. I went through the bathroom industry like a whirlwind, becoming the best I could be by learning and teaching myself along the way. By always telling myself I was the best and believing I was, my bathroom career flourished. I did develop my skill as a bathroom designer and my communication skills improved as well and all through hard work, dedication and belief. It wasn't long before others started to notice my confidence and the sales I was bringing in for my company. I became in demand with all the other bathroom companies as they all tried to poach me away which helped to build my confidence.

The moment of truth came when I had a life-changing decision to make. I had been approached by one of the biggest bathroom companies in the UK to take a very high paying management role, but at the same time my current boss had offered me a chance to buy the business from him and become my own boss. What was I to do?

I was ready, and it was my time to shine and to prove to myself, and so many others, that I had what it takes to be successful. I was strong enough, and I believed in myself enough to take things to the next level. Throughout my years as the co-owner of Watford Bathrooms and Kitchens self-belief and affirmations have played a massive part in my success. There are so many ups and downs, and if I didn't tell myself every day how capable I am and reaffirm that, I would not be here telling my story. The amount of times I have had to stand in front of that mirror to say, you can do this, you have what it takes, is untrue, but without that self-belief, that passion and desire you let the world and others take over. I don't want that to happen to me, and I doubt you do too.

The repetition of affirmations is crucial to your life, no matter what you are doing or what you want to achieve. You have to realise you are awesome and truly believe it. I assure you that every great inventor, speaker, author, sportsman, stockbroker or whatever business someone is in, they will use self-affirmations. If you ever wanted proof of self-affirmation, you need to look no further than the walking affirmation himself "Muhammad Ali," with his phrase "I am the greatest, I said that even before I knew I was." Look at what that man achieved with self-belief and by not letting anyone else decide what his future held.

My life and my day would not work if I did not repeat my self-affirmations, as this is a consistent action required to achieve your ultimate dreams. This action will influence and activate the subconscious mind into positive action. You become what you think.

The Gazza Bounce Self Affirmation Guide.

When done correctly, self-affirmations can, and will, change your attitude and behaviours. You will stay focused and add motivation to achieving your dreams for as long as you make this a daily habit in your life.

- Create your own definite phrases, making them powerful and meaningful to you. Make them effective in your daily routines.
- Write them down and make them visible, so you do not forget until they are imbedded deep into your subconscious mind.
- Only use positive words.
- Always do this first thing in the morning and at least twice more throughout the day (be brave and shout them out).
- Make sure you are showing all the passion, desire and conviction when saying them. Belief and enthusiasm is key to this working.
- You need to live them and make sure you practise what you affirm.
- Repetition of your affirmations creates the ultimate self-belief.

Chapter 5

Fuelling your mind

You are probably getting a very strong idea from this book that I was not very good at school and although it wasn't my greatest strength the real question was, was my mind being fuelled properly?

I have a short attention span and get bored easily, but there must be a very good reason for this surely? I am sitting here writing my book so what does that say or, furthermore, what does that mean? I found the ability to learn and, although my spelling and grammar could be better, I have been successful in many other areas of my life.

Reaching the age of 37 years old, I fully understand the power of self-development; if you make something that is engaging and grabs my attention, I will sit and want to learn it. I cannot believe how passionate I am now for fuelling my mind, but if I know it is going to enhance my self-development and open new doors I will grab it with both hands.

Let's travel back in time again to my early days, making it out of the bathroom warehouse and onto the showroom floor. We had two floor managers, an assistant manager, a sales assistant and then me. I had nagged my boss for ages about wanting to get into the showroom and out of the warehouse (you have to remember I was destined for greatness) and that time had come. I had to prove I was better than everyone else and I could do this because no matter what, I wasn't going back to being a warehouse boy. Now I had a purpose and the desire to succeed. The only way that this was going to happen was that I had to fuel my mind. I had to get up to speed with all the products being sold, the prices they were sold at as well as all the technical information that I needed to know.

My goal was to learn all the brochures inside out. I had to know this stuff really well, and I had to be determined. I also had to have total faith in my abilities and truly believe I could do this. I took home every single brochure with me, and I studied them as if it was a university degree. It ate into my social life, but I persisted, and I could feel the results. Along with all the product information, I had to develop people skills, sales and presentation techniques. The way to do this was by studying everyone else and how they approached clients. I modelled everyone but took the best from each of them to form my own style.

Soon I was flying, the sales were coming in, and my confidence was growing daily. The next challenge I faced was having to step it up a notch and start learning how to do the actual designing. Although I was becoming good at sales, I knew the managers were earning the top money because they could offer the clients the full service and deal with the developers and architects.

At this stage remember I was still very young and money was a huge driver in my life; I wanted nice clothes and to enjoy my weekends to the max. For that to happen, I had to up my game which meant I had to fuel my mind to get even better. It was a dual effect; as I enhanced my knowledge, I was increasing my income as well. What I also learnt was that I was creating value and by value, I mean my worth to the company. I was also gaining ambition. I wanted to be number one in the showroom.

I pushed myself and started to learn about colour schemes, studying architectural plans and drawings so that I could understand scales and rules. The hardest part of all the learning was the drawing of bathrooms by hand and having to present that as an idea to a potential client. No challenge was too much though when you have a goal. I was learning, and things were exciting. I had something to aim for, namely the money and the Dolce & Gabbana designer clothes in the shop opposite the showroom. Even thinking about it now, I remember that I had my very own personal goal wall that I could look at every single day to remind me why I was pushing myself so hard.

Once again I had done it, I achieved the knowledge that was required, and soon I was getting the clients I wanted and, by increasing my skillset, I was seriously increasing my value and worth. The most important thing to remember is that I was doing this for myself and no one else. I was entirely self-centred in that I wanted these things for me, but in return, the company was making more money too. It was a win-win situation.

I went on to become one of the best in my field and became an in-demand bathroom designer with other showrooms constantly offering me packages to leave where I was. It was at this point that I decided it was time to start my own business. If it was not for all the hard work, determination and the pure desire to succeed, this might never have happened. I knew that the only way forward in my life was to take on this next challenge, this next level of self-development, as at that point I realised if I wanted to make something of myself the only person that could do it was me.

The fuelling didn't stop there as my skills were only going to get me so far when it came to running my own business. You see, I stopped learning for nearly two years once I opened the business because I thought I had made it. I mean, I owned my own business, didn't I? That means I'm a success surely? How wrong could someone be? However, I understand why people get caught out like this; thinking they are good at something and can just start up a business and everything will be awesome. The fact is they are wrong, and so was I.

I was only going to survive for so long by being good at bathroom design and selling bathrooms, and I learnt this the hard way, by nearly losing everything. I used to think "Why am I not getting any customers? I have a showroom, I have a website, I'm in the yellow pages, and I even have ads in some posh magazines." Nothing happened though, the tumbleweed continued to tumble past my showroom windows, something had to change, and it had to change drastically, the hard part was the realisation that it was me that had to change. The million dollar question was, "How?"

I didn't have a mentor. Everything I had learnt so far was self-taught, and the emotional drivers came flooding back, with all of my teachers telling me I was a failure. The surprise was that was exactly what I needed. It was when the "GazzaBounce" sprang back into action, and I started looking at ways to develop myself and step up a gear.

I discovered business networking which became a great life skill for me and set me on a new journey which opened up so many new doors. It also introduced me to some great people, but I think what I learnt most from this was how to present myself and speak in public. I had to learn how to stand up in front 30-50 people and tell them about my business. I was so nervous; standing up and delivering a speech for sixty seconds used to scare the hell out of me. I would shake as it got closer to being my turn to stand up. I turned this into a new form of learning though and it became a process because I had to do it every week. I would make sure I prepared, and I learnt how to deal with the pressure.

I would also attend presentation workshops to learn new techniques and methods of delivering my message. That was when my true self started to shine through along with my confidence. This also helped me improve my sales skills, which lead to greater conversion rates within my business and introduced me to great new contacts. The business networking could only take me so far though, and I knew I had to learn more.

This is where my love affair started with "The Entrepreneurs Circle" and where my life moved to a completely new level with self-development and business skills. It was the ultimate learning resource, and that continues to this day. They taught me the most amazing new things that always kept my business at the forefront. The skills I learn on a daily basis are immense, and that is backed up by the amazing new people I surrounded myself with.

When you surround yourself with the right people, all you want to do is learn from them. It becomes a source of inspiration because if you are the smartest person in the room, you need to find a new room and quick. The vast number of different and amazing people I surround myself with keeps me developing, and I have never been so focused in my life. When you have these people around you, they are always discussing a different book they have read or a different technique they have used within their business. Even their own experiences help enhance me because you are so engulfed with what they have to say. It's pure respect, and that keeps feeding and fuelling the mind.

This is where I have to mention the great man that is Nigel Botterill, the creator of "The Entrepreneurs Circle". He is a marketing genius in my eyes, and when Nigel talks, you listen. It's as simple as that. Nigel has created this tool, this platform, where if you just follow the steps and listen, your business will grow tenfold. The other thing I would go as far as saying is that he has created the ultimate family and the reason I say this is because he created a unity amongst business people and entrepreneurs. We know that within this community, we can turn to each other and ask for help, whether it be of a business nature or personal, and that's the power of surrounding yourself with like-minded people driven by the need to better themselves through learning and developing. This information supplied by Nigel is the main reason that my business is still here after eight years and probably why I still have this burning desire to continue to succeed. Because these tools are being shared by Nigel and "The Entrepreneurs Circle" I'm even more excited now than the first day I started my business as I know the more I develop myself, the easier it will become to achieve my dreams.

This is also true for anyone else. Here you have a man who got thrown out of school, who started working in the back of a bathroom warehouse, to running his own business, to writing this book and sharing his story so that others can realise their dreams and understand anything is possible if you're willing to learn. I am sitting on my sofa following my heart, stepping out of my comfort zone and reaching my dreams all because of the power of self-development. It's simple if I can do it, so can you. It's true that sacrifices have to be made, but you have to look at the results, look at what could be achieved if you did the hard work now. Don't wish life was easier, wish you were better.

By taking the time to read this book, and other books you are taking giant steps and I cannot emphasise enough how important it is for your bounce in life, to continue to learn and educate yourself in the right areas. You need to keep following your dreams and developing your mind, no matter what happens in life. Once you have that knowledge, no one can ever take it away. With knowledge, you can overcome anything that life has to throw at you. They can take your house, they can take your car, they can take the clothes off your back, but as long as you are developing and fuelling your mind, you will just keep coming back stronger and better than ever before. Please remember that life was not meant to be easy, so do the hard stuff now to make the future easier. You can never know too much and the more you develop, the more you get to learn about yourself and your WHY in life. You begin to discover your purpose in life and what you actually want from it. This is where you get to choose your future because it's your choice where you want to go and what you choose to let enter your mind.

There are so many different levels of self-development, but fuelling the mind has been my ultimate key to success because you can learn about anything and for me that has helped me overcome so many obstacles, fears and challenges on my journey to discovering that greatness within.

51

Chapter 6

Jumping out of bed and your comfort zone

The problem with the majority of people is that they follow the whims of the world and its daily actions and the problem with that is that it makes them the same as everybody else. It is a wonderful thing to want to be secure but a tragedy to be too scared to see what else is out there.

I promise I won't labour the point too much, but schools do not help with this situation because of the system we are taught to follow. We go through our whole youth being told to do well in school, get good grades so that you can then get a really good job, buy a house and hopefully you will excel at your job, get a good pension, retire and then eventually die gracefully and happy. Keep following the conveyor belt of life, and you will lead a long and successful life. Here is my big "BUT" and question about this. What about "ME" and the thousands of other kids that didn't get on too well with school and align with that conveyor belt? What path are we all supposed to follow? What conveyor belt are they suggesting we get on and off of? It's simple really. They don't have an answer; it's a case of "don't know, don't care." That's ok though because we have own little secret stuck up our sleeves and all it needs is a little encouragement. The secret is "PASSION", "DETERMINATION" and the fire that burns in our belly that says "I don't care what you think about me because it is none of my business".

What thousands of kids, and I know, is that if we are willing to take a gamble, if we are willing to step out of our comfort zones, then just maybe there is a whole new world out there waiting to be explored.

All through my life, I have had to step outside of my comfort zones to better myself, but as I grew older and wiser, I realised how powerful a tool that really is because change creates opportunities like you can't believe. One of the biggest challenges most of us have to face is that when we leave school, we have to get a job. That's a scary thing when all you have known is the safety of school. Like so many others, I accepted it and got on with it.

There was also the football for me. I could have stayed with certain clubs, being the best player in the team and taken the accolades week in and out, but I wanted to prove to myself that I could play at a higher level and I did.

The next part of my life was probably the defining moment in my life because if I didn't decide to step out of my comfort zone, I wouldn't be sitting here in Doncaster writing this part of my book. (I will explain later why I'm in Doncaster!)

Earlier I explained how I excelled at bathroom design and sales and how I went on to own the company. Before that happened I had an inspiring, but scary defining moment in my life's journey. It all came from a meeting with my dad (this will be the first he knows about this). I don't think he has ever realised how important and defining his words were and why, to this day, I live every single moment as I do now.

Before deciding to become self-employed and buy my own business, I visited my dad and wanted his opinion on what he thought I should do. This how the conversation went. "Dad, I've been offered the chance to buy my own business or take a very secure job on a very high earning wage. The easy option is obviously to take the money, but I feel I there is more to me than just working for someone else."

My dad replied, "Gary, being your own boss isn't easy, but if you do right it it can be very self-rewarding. What is your gut telling you?" he asked

"To go for it and start creating my own future, but I'm so scared," I replied, and I really was.

"What are you scared of?" He was genuinely concerned, but I could also tell that he was supportive. It was exactly what I needed at the moment.

"You mean what have I got to lose?" I wanted to be precise with my replies. "I could lose my house, my home!"

His response surprised me "That's just a pile of bricks son if it goes wrong so what? You lose your house, and you start again and buy another one."

There was a very long pause before I said anything.

"I suppose so, I hadn't looked at it that way," I said; a light switched on inside of me, and I knew which decision to make. I smashed the walls down of my comfort zone and said: "Sod it, let's do this."

I signed on the dotted line and started a brand new chapter in my life to create my future and to take responsibility for all of my actions. I have often wondered where I would be if I hadn't had that conversation so this is another part of the book where I say to my dad, "I love you" and thank him for creating such a strong mind shift in my life. That conversation changed my life forever.

There have been many more changes that I have had to make, but having the power of my dad's words always in my ear along with the passion and desire to succeed, I have been able to make those decisions that many are just too scared to make. It is also important to say that I have made some very seriously stupid and bad decisions along the way as well. They hurt my business and my personal life, but they were still decisions that I had to make. I have always seen failure as a stepping stone to succeeding, and without failure in your life, you cannot move forward.

I don't have to reel off a list of great people that have failed in life before they achieved greatness, because if you are reading my book, you know this already and you get it, you understand me. But more importantly you understand the power of failure, and you are ready to challenge yourself and smash down your walls and truly bounce high out of your comfort zone.

Another story that I hold very close to my heart is a comfort zone that I cannot believe I broke out of, but I am so proud of myself for doing this as this holds something even more personal. First of all, I wanted to share what led to actually doing this. I had just had one of my breakdowns and was in a very bad place and a low point in my life. This was my first experience of a breakdown, so it completely threw me. I am always full of energy and bouncing so high on life, but for whatever the reason, life had got on top of me, personally and from my business. I fell hard, and it was the strangest feeling I have ever felt. This is where family and friends play a massive part in your life in getting you back on track. Once again this is an opportunity to say a very special and massive thank you to all my family, my wife Linda and three truly inspirational friends: Chris Musgrove, Darryl Bertie and Marie Cross. Not only did they support me, but they also showed me another path which led me to get focused onto something that was a little crazy but fun at the same time.

I needed to get myself into something that was going pick me up and get that bounce back, and this is where The Entrepreneurs Circle had a big event coming up called 'Sex Sells.' This was an event about marketing techniques and how you can use sexual suggestion and flirty marketing to help promote your business. The problem I had was that I only had eight weeks actually to accomplish it.

My idea was could I get myself super fit and get my body into the best shape of my life, then turn up to this event practically naked? This would require some serious commitment, passion, desire and certainly big balls (if you know what I mean) because this was definitely out of my comfort zone. What have I got to lose though? Other than my dignity and pride of course!

Even the thought of this was so damn scary I had the right mindset to know I could pull it off; this was a completely different level of stepping out of my comfort zone, even for me. The only way I was going to achieve this was to get some help and the man to help me was Aaron Philips from FitStart UK. I asked him if this was achievable as we only had eight weeks to make it happen. Aaron had complete faith in his abilities but did warn me that he would only take it on if I accepted his rules. This meant sweat, blood and tears and I had to do exactly what he said. I accepted.

Aaron put me on very strict dietary plans along with training schedules that pushed me to the limits. Change was not the word for what I was doing; these were not just comfort zone walls I had to climb, these were bloody mountains to overcome. True to his word, and with my determination, we did it, and I truly was in the best shape of my life.

The next comfort zone I had to step out of was just weird, so no laughing as I explain this part without cringing myself! I had to shave and *Imac* every last hair off my body except for my head and eyebrows and follow that up with a spray tan. I had decided that no matter what I was going to achieve my goal and this was all part of it.

Now I am looking quite buff, if I say so myself and it's time to rock up to this "Sex Sells" event in Bolton. When I turned up the night before I had to make sure my whole body was covered up so that no one suspected what I had done. I even had to tell a few white lies and say I had just been on holiday when people mentioned how tanned I was. The big reveal came the following morning.

The event is now here, and with just a few hours away it's 4am and I am actually shitting myself. I'm so scared and nervous, but there is to be no turning back; I had come this far, and it's time to see this through. I waited for the gym to open at 6am so I can get down there and get myself focused and keep my mind straight before the big reveal. After a brief workout I'm back in my room and laid out on the bed is my outfit: a hard hat, the skimpiest pair of jean shorts you can imagine and my tool belt of course. I am your sexy dream plumber feeling hot and ready for action. I even got myself a big fake tattoo across my very toned stomach saying "Watford Bathrooms and Kitchens." I'm now ready to face everyone. I took a deep breath and walked out the door with Linda, and I went for it.

Bearing in mind this was not a fancy dress event the reaction was unbelievable. With everyone else in normal clothes, you could say I stood out. I smashed it and kicked down my barriers; not because I looked so good but because I had achieved my goal. I had set a new standard for comfort zones and knew I could achieve even more. I got so much from this experience, and the biggest thing was being acknowledged by my mentor, Nigel Botterill. He got me up on the stage in front of everyone; for the rest of the day people wanted their pictures taken with me, and the following month I won the National Entrepreneur of the Month award. As you can imagine how much I was buzzing because I had the "brass balls" to change something and step out of my comfort zone and be different to everyone else.

The reason I wanted to share these stories is to help you understand that you can come back from your setbacks. It's not what happens, but how you react to these situations that will always define your true character.

I fell hard and truly hard like you couldn't imagine, but I fell on my back, which meant I was looking up and if you can look up, you can get up and that's exactly what I did. Of course, I had great people around me to help, but I still did it, I made that decision, that choice that I was better than the situation and I turned it into a positive and I bounced the hell out of it. I chose to change my habits and take consistent action to achieve my goals, I broke my goals down into bite size chunks and kept pushing and pushing until I reached the top of my very own mountain. I climbed those steps just like *Rocky Balboa* did. No matter what your situation, don't you ever let it be an excuse to stop trying.

My George Clarke Experience.

As you already know, I have travelled to Doncaster to listen to George Clarke speak so I thought I would share my experience with you and how that made me feel. At this moment I have aspirations to be just like George, but in the bathroom world on TV. I feel there is a gap in the market that can be filled and it certainly would make good TV because everyone loves an awesome looking bathroom. This is just another vision and dream I have, but you must set your goals so big that they scare you.

The morning of seeing George was a little bit nerve-racking, as I felt like I was there for completely different reasons compared to everybody else. I was there to hear what he had to say so that maybe I could learn and add something that would help me on my journey towards my goal. When George started talking, I was fixated and listened intently; I wanted to hear how it all started and how his journey began and how he got to where he is now. Which was exactly what he talked about!

His journey began as a very young boy, and he had a dream that he wanted to pursue. Like all of us he had his knockbacks, but he showed his persistence, and by not giving up, George found the opportunity that he craved for. His world opened up which in turn gave George the desire to achieve all he aimed for.

61

Don't Be A Goose

After reaching a very high level in his career, George was asked to write a book not realising is that the publicist was also involved in TV. She saw George as a great candidate as a presenter for a new TV programme they were trying to launch. He wasn't keen at first but after a lot of persuasion went along and he absolutely smashed it. He was offered the part and has never looked back.

He has also been able to use his influence to do great things for charities and kids that haven't had the start or chances in life that they deserved. I took so much from George's speech, and it so resonated with me; I felt truly inspired.

After he had finished his talk, he did a little walk around and then it was book signing time. I was really excited as I was going to get my chance to have a brief chat with him about my goals and aspirations. I had just been in a big national bathroom and kitchens magazine called *KandBNews* and had a big three-page article written about me and the business including my ambitions. Believe it or not, the headline they had used was "I want to be the George Clarke of bathrooms" so I wasn't going to miss the opportunity for that to be signed by him.

As I stood in the queue, excited like a little school kid holding my magazine, my turn came around, and George looked up at me and says, 'I have been expecting you, Gary.' We both had a giggle, and I let him know that we all have dreams and there is no point having small dreams. It was an amazing personal feeling because George had taken the time to read my article, he knew who I was, and he wrote a great personal message for me, along with signing it. That made me feel about ten feet tall and just reaffirmed what an amazing and inspirational man he is. By now it was time for me to go home. I'd had a great day but as I was heading for the train station, guess who I bump into? Only George, we had a little chat, he called me a stalker (in a nice way!), and we went our separate ways.

It just shows what an effect certain people can have on your life. Aspiring to be someone or like someone can create a massive drive and purpose in your life. It certainly has for me, as you have already figured out. Never give up on pursuing something you are passionate about, especially your dreams, because anything is possible if you are willing to do stuff the others won't. I took upon myself to learn more about George because he is doing something that I aspire to do and that is the point here. There will always be someone who has done what you are trying to do, so find out how they did it, what drove them and what they had to sacrifice to make their dreams come true. I followed my heart because I want to achieve greatness, so what is stopping you from doing the same?

Chapter 7

The dreams and goal effect

It is vital to understand the importance of having goals and dreams; it shocks me to hear people not having a purpose in life, and it upsets me. It's so painful to hear because of the world and environments we are brought up in. We are taught by so many people not to dream and, for me, that is appalling. It's time to stop listening to others and start listening to yourself; it is only you who should get to decide and choose what is right for you and what's next for your future. If you want to dream, do it but just make sure it's not just a dream. Make sure you are going to do something about it and take consistent action in achieving your dreams.

You know that feeling when you close your eyes, and you imagine the best version of you possible, that person who is living the life that you feel you should have? That's the person you really are, so it's time to face yourself and let go of that part of you that doesn't truly believe.

The first step to getting what you want is having the courage to get rid of the things you don't want. You have choices to make when you wake up in the morning. You can either put your head back on the pillow, pull the quilt tight and continue to sleep with your dreams or wake up and bounce out of bed and start chasing them.

Having goals and dreams in life have made me realise what is important to me, I have something to aim for, a certain level of success and expectation for myself and for my family. The remarkable thing about goals and dreams is that they can always change and they can always be updated. However, don't dream small and never give up!

The key element of having goals is to make sure they are written down; make them visual so that they can be accessed and seen every single day of your life. They need to be in your face so that you can reaffirm why you're bouncing out of bed every morning and doing what you are doing. By not writing these down and keeping them in your head all that happens is they stay fantasies and just something you might get round to one day if you can be bothered.

Take action right here and right now, write down your wildest dreams and don't you dare hold back; see what an amazing feeling it is just to write down what you really want out of life. You will be amazed by the way you feel when you start to visualise what could be. Many people talk about the graveyard being the richest place in the world because so many people die and take their dreams to their deathbeds.

Don't let this be you; there is no reason in the world to stop you from achieving greatness; get them out of your head and start creating your future.

I have all my dreams written down on a massive whiteboard in my office at home which I look at every morning and every evening. I have them written down in my notepad, and I have also taken a picture of them so that I know they are in my pocket everywhere I go, to remind myself why I'm working so hard and what the end rewards are going to be for myself and my family.

One of the most important things to do is to let people know what your dreams are. Telling people your dreams makes you accountable to them and your actions. You can't say to someone "In six months' time I'm going to have a new car" and then when six months comes around you still haven't achieved it, can you? You would look silly especially if you haven't made any effort to make it happen.

This has been my biggest spur to achieve my goals because I tell everyone I know, that mine are going to happen. I love the pressure of knowing I cannot give up, that I'm going to prove to myself I can achieve greatness. I believe in myself enough to make these bold statements, I believe and know everything on my whiteboard is going to happen because I have the desire in me to do just that.

Of course, you can't just turn around and say I want to be rich because it has no purpose, it has no driver. To achieve each goal you need to put smaller goals in place, as I did, which drove me closer each day towards my ultimate goal. They may be baby steps, but at least I know every day I'm edging closer to making the big dream a reality. I have broken down my dreams into sections:

- Personal Development
- Life Goals
- Toys
- Business
- Finance
- Family
- Personal Dream

By doing this it helps me define what category my dreams and goals fall under, this was taught to me by my business coach Parag Prasad from Action Coach. He taught me never to hold back, and that is why I am sitting here encouraging you to do the same.

You need to write down what you want as if money was no object, what would you want out of those seven headings. This has to be one of the biggest influences of my life and still has that massive effect to this day. Think big!

I just had to pause and take another look up at my whiteboard and see my dreams while I'm writing this because having them there in front of me shows that I have a purpose in life, I truly understand where I want my life to be and which direction I'm travelling in.

Another really good way of looking at this is something that virtually everybody has done in their lifetime. No matter how much money people have, a holiday is always top of their own goal's list even if it is in their heads. This is something that pretty much always happens because no matter what, they always find the money to go away. You create your goal: 'The holiday.' You work your arse off to raise the money needed, you work day and night because of the excitement of the end result, the reward and eventually you get there. The end goal is always worth the work and the sense of satisfaction you get from achieving your goal is amazing. Ask yourself, how many times in your life have you had that feeling? Anything is possible if you put your mind to it.

When you have dreams it is crucial that you surround yourself with the right people because so many friends and family will shoot you down and tell you that it is just not possible and why are you even bothering? This is when your mindset has to stay strong, and the goal has to be a powerful enough driver. You have to believe in yourself to tell them that you are going to achieve this goal no matter what. Being a part of Action Coach and The Entrepreneurs Circle has put me alongside the type of people who have dreams, and I have had the pleasure of watching these people blossom just as they have with me.

The biggest challenge you will face is "SACRIFICE". It is impossible to reach your dreams or complete your goals without certain sacrifices. For some people, these are going to be completely different to others, but it is a hurdle you have to get over. This is a mindset issue and a hurdle that so many fall at because they don't have the willpower to force them over or the bounce to lift them as high as they need to jump to get them closer to that dream. Just like my "Sex Sells" story I told you about earlier; I had to make sacrifices, the tasty, delicious food and drinks that I wasn't allowed so I could make sure I reached my goal. The result was worth it though!

My ultimate challenge this year was sacrificing certain friends because I love socialising and I had to give up going to parties, going on stag do's because it what was needed to happen to make sure I stayed on track to achieving my vision and my goals.

On the 20th December 2014, I had my own vision, a goal, a dream, so I had to make sure all my priorities were in place, and I had to be 100% focused, and that's what I did. There were many friends and family members that tried to deter my focus, but I stayed so strong and still to this day I am 100% committed to my cause, to my family and to my friends. I still reflect and look at where I am today because I am a completely different person to who I was a year ago. The reason I say that is because I was brave enough to dream.

For a start here I am writing a book, proving to myself and showing so many others that anything is possible. If I can do this then so can you! The proof is in the pudding, as they say, a cold stone fact. I have people watching my "GazzaBounce" motivational videos and sending me cards thanking me for helping them through certain days. They tell me that I inspire them to take action with their lives and get them through tough times.

Another major lesson is to understand the process of working on your dreams. There will be many setbacks, but this is where you truly start to discover who you really are, what your capabilities are and what you are made of. Too many people don't believe in themselves enough.

I have a saying, and that is "DON'T BE A GOOSE". I liked it so much I named the book after it. The reason I say this is because all geese fly in the same direction, they all take off and follow each other because that's what geese do. Could you imagine if one of those geese decided one day that they fancied being a little different and instead of following the same flock year after year and seeing the same places and getting the same results every time? Could you imagine if one goose had a dream? What if that goose decided to fly in a different direction? He could end up on the coolest island he had ever been to with all these hot, sexy, cool other geese were living their dreams.

Another path could lead to a land of opportunities, so don't be scared as it is your duty to dream. It's necessary for you to choose your future but to do that you must have a dream.

The world is full of complainers; people who moan about their situation and make up excuses as to why they are where they are. Most of the time it is never their fault, it's always someone else's. But guess what? They won't do anything about it; they won't pick up a book or listen to an audio to enhance their life, they just moan. What makes you different, why you are full of bounce, is because you are an uncommon breed. You have aspirations to do something and you will take action immediately. So today is that day!

I had a dream, and that was to inspire others to believe in themselves. Remember this: no dream you can ever have will ever be too far-fetched as long as you are willing to work for it. Now ask yourself the ultimate no-brainer question? How bad do you want it? Write down the goal and just bloody go for it.

What my dream looks like.

So after sharing my insights to dreams and goals, I thought it would be good to share with you where I am at this moment in time. And the best way for me to do that is to sit here and write what my dream looks like and where I will be in three years' time.

My business will be running on its own and it will be self-sufficient. This will mean that I have finally reached the financial number that I had set myself to give me the freedom and the opportunity to either carry on being a business owner or sell the business and start looking for new ventures. I would have firmly established the brand that is Gary Fullwood and opened up the doors within the TV sector which will be ready to host my new bathroom show. This TV show is all about the real experiences of having your bathroom supplied and installed; it will be aimed to show people the realities of what is needed to make sure you get the desired results for what you paid for. This is to take the illusions away from all the budget TV shows that make having a bathroom installed really easy and cheap. I will have built up my reputation enough that I will be endorsing bathroom products all over the country and putting a stamp on products that have my core values within them. I will also have launched my independent designer franchise and helped hundreds of bathroom and kitchen designers realise their dreams of going out on their own and creating wealth for themselves.

I will also be travelling around the country inspiring other likeminded people looking to take their lives to the next level with motivational speaking sessions as well as creating a "Mastermind" group for the bathroom and kitchen sector.

Away from the business I would have been on my way to helping fostered children get the start and education they deserve with aspirations to make this a much larger force and organisation. I will also have the beautiful Georgian family home I want, and the extra family time I would have created for myself. Going on family holidays but also the luxury holidays for just me and Linda (the wife). I will have also reach the dream of driving around in my brand new Range Rover Autobiography (black with white trim).

Let's see what my day looks like when I wake each day in this goal state:

Its 5am and I wake up to a very quiet "Fullwood" household, so I creep out of bed without waking Linda, grabbing my shorts and jumper. I get downstairs to the awesome greeting of my very bouncy dog Titus and open the double doors to my Cornwall summer house. I look out onto the beautiful beach and go for a walk with Titus, taking in the amazing morning. As daylight starts to break through, I get my phone out and start to prepare this morning's Gazza Bounce TV. Once that is done I head back to see my family, wake up and chill out while eating my breakfast.

After getting ready Linda, Titus and I jump in the car ready for our drive to go and start filming on one of my TV episodes. After a few hours of filming, I have an appointment with a section of business owners from one of my "Mastermind" sessions. These are always a crucial part of the day as this is where I was a few years back being inspired by others and helping me get into the position I am now.

Once I'm back on the road with Linda, we make the call to the "Fostered Children Organisation" we are helping, to make sure everything is going according to plan and preparing the next steps that are required.

Finally, it's time to head back to the Georgian home to have a nice family dinner with all the kids and share the stories of the day.

Let's not forget how important it is to keep dreaming and creating goals once you have reached certain levels because there are always other levels for ourselves that need to be reached as well as giving back and inspiring others.

Chapter 8

My Journey So Far

I wanted to share where I am in my life so far and what I have had to do to get to this point in my life. I want you to understand why I'm writing this book; The journey I am on is still at its beginning stages and proving that anything is possible if you believe in yourself and have the desires to follow your dreams, but obviously, it is still continuous.

I have recently hit a huge milestone in my life through making some massive sacrifices to get there. This milestone might not be massive to some of you, but to me, it has become a gigantic measure of what can be achieved. I hope it inspires you, to hear what a warehouse boy with no qualifications can do when you put your mind to something.

On the 20th December 2014, I sat on my bathroom showroom floor and cried to myself as my life was in a total shit place (sorry for the language). I was not with Linda due to breaking up in June, and my business was well over fifty thousand pounds in debt. I sat there not knowing how I was going to overcome this situation and also not knowing where my next customers were going come from. I had no goals written down that year as I was not in control due to the breakdown of my marriage. After feeling sorry for myself, I decided to make that commitment and share my worries; I needed to tell someone what was going on because I knew I was better than this. I had worked too hard all my life to let my life slip through my fingers. I have been a fighter all my life and had too many knockbacks, so why should this be different to any of my other challenges in life?

I phoned a very good friend of mine. We'll call him "Wayne," and he will know who he is. I explained my situation. Wayne soon told me how it is and explained about his battles and said 'It's not how hard you fall, it's how you get back up and move forward.' So after a kick up the arse from Wayne, I then spoke to Marie Cross as I needed to hear a more tender side as well.

Marie is an amazing woman who has inspired me for years; I have seen her rise from ashes, and she gave me the wise but caring words that showed me that I could rise again. It was decision time and drastic changes needed to be made. I began by getting Linda back; this had to be the start of my journey as I needed to be home and my two boys needed a settled environment. With stage one complete I was now home with Linda and back home with my two boys and my stepson. Awesome!!

The next important stage was to stop drinking completely. I'm not a big drinker anyway but if I was going to be laser-focused, I had to take that part of my life away. This was probably my biggest challenge if I'm completely honest as I had to stop hanging around with certain friends. That meant there could be no distractions. Sacrificing certain friends was very hard as I love my partying; many of them couldn't understand what I was doing but as long as I did and I had the backing of Linda and my boys that was all that mattered at this stage in my life. Stage two complete, no drinking and stop hanging around with people who are not helping me reach my goals.

The next stage, after getting advice from Wayne and Marie, was to get a business coach. This was crucial as I needed accountability and the right tools to get my business back on track. It was very expensive but exactly what I needed. This is where I met Parag Prasad from Action Coach; he was inspiring and had the credentials to get me back on track within my business and beyond. Parag's group coaching sessions have empowered me to move forward, and it didn't take long before I was back setting my goals and crossing them off my list. Stage three complete, business coaching well underway.

Stage four was to make sure I was surrounded by the right people, those to inspire me to move forward. This wasn't hard part to complete as I knew exactly where I had to go to make this happen. I made a call to my very good friend Darryl Bertie (from the Entrepreneurs Circle) about getting seriously involved again. He welcomed me with open arms, and I started my new journey with truly inspiring likeminded people alongside me. I made sure I was part of what they call the "Inside Track" as so many people I knew where a part of this higher inner level and that's where I needed to be.

Every person in the "EC" understands what it's like to be where I was, so it was easy to talk about the problems in my life. Stage four complete; by surrounding myself with inspirational and likeminded people it helping me to closer to my goals and dreams.

Stage five was self-affirmations, this was a game changer for me. I decided I needed to be getting up every single morning and telling myself how awesome I was and what I was capable of achieving. I would get up and pull silly faces in the mirror and scream how good I was, then take Titus for a walk saying the same things over and over again. Other dog walkers must have thought I was nuts! It worked for me though so why would I care what others think of me? It's none of my business at the end of the day!

To reaffirm this, I would post positive quotes on Instagram, Facebook and Pinterest. This made me feel really good, but it wasn't enough; I needed more accountability, so I made a crazy decision to start filming myself doing these self-affirmations and posting them on YouTube and social media. This meant that I had to practice what I was preaching.

It had a dramatic life effect as I started to realise that I was helping others. How empowering is that? People were watching me and taking notice and making better life decisions of their own. I remember stopping after a couple of months, and my phone and messages went crazy, people were telling me they needed their "GazzaBounce" fix in the mornings and would I carry on? Not only was I getting my life back on track, but I was also inspiring others! Stage five complete, self-affirmations well underway and driving my self-belief through the roof.

Stage six was about getting shit done! After sitting in a room with Nigel Botterill and hearing him talk about ninety minutes for about the thousandth time, it finally sank in. If a man of Nigel's stature is getting up earlier than most people and spending ninety minutes working on his business before his day to day work schedule starts, why the hell aren't I?

From that day I got up earlier, and after my self-affirmations, I'm working on my business for ninety minutes, not in it, before my normal day starts. This has impacted my business tenfold, and the results are coming in.

If you run a business and you are not doing this yourself, stop reading, quickly get your diary up and put in ninety-minute chunks every day! It doesn't need to be in the morning; it's important this goes in your diary when you feel you are at your peak! Not everyone is stupidly happy and effective like I am at 5:30am in the mornings; that's my peak bounciest, and when my brain is ready to attack any challenges and obstacle I might have. Your time might be different, but please start doing it. I am getting so much shit done; you wouldn't believe. Stage six complete, getting shit done because I'm spending ninety minutes a day working on my business and not in it!

Stage seven, education and reading. I have always enjoyed reading and listening to audiobooks since my entrepreneur journey began. It's been crucial to where I am now because if you are not learning, you are not earning. My car is now what I call "My Automobile University" (I did nick that from the legendary Zig Ziglar), but I no longer listen to music in the mornings, only inspirational and motivational audios. When a new book is recommended to me, I'm on it, and I'm reading and have nearly got myself to a position where I'm either listening or reading a book a week. Everything I listen to or read gives me something, even if it is just one golden nugget; that is all I need to help me get to the next level. Stage seven complete, reading more and educating myself.

After explaining seven of my stages, I can sit here and tell you that last week my bookkeeper called me into my office to tell me that I no longer owe anyone any money! Of course, I still have my monthly expenses like everybody else, but I do not owe anyone any money! I have no loans hanging over me, and I have no suppliers chasing me for money. That is a milestone for me, and it is why I'm so proud to sit here and tell you that story. It's completely relevant as to why I wanted to write this book. Not only have I paid off all my debts, but I'm running a company successfully and getting new clients in so I can keep building and creating my future.

Within ten months I have turned my life around all because I truly believed in myself and my abilities, while not forgetting it could not have been done without the amazing and inspirational people I surrounded myself with. If you use my seven stages, it can work for you as well.

One of my favourite stories "The Chinese Bamboo Tree."

This truly sums me and my journey up and once you have read this you I hope you can relate to it as well.

In the Far East, they have something that called the "Chinese Bamboo Tree"; this tree takes five years to grow, and when they go through the process of growing it, they have to water and fertilise the ground where it has been placed, every single day without fail. The tree itself doesn't break through the ground until the fifth year, but once it breaks through the ground, within five weeks, it grows ninety feet tall. The danger was in the growing time: if that person had stopped watering and nurturing and fertilising that dream, that bamboo tree would have died in the ground. You imagine all the people talking and watching that man watering the ground, and nothing is happening whatsoever. "What you doing there fella? You have been out here a very long time my man, everyone is talking about you and they are saying you're growing some sort of Chinese bamboo tree, is that right? The problem is my man; everyone can see that there is nothing there, everyone thinks you're crazy!" Isn't that true in life? People can't see past the obstacles. They are asking how long you been working on your dream? And still, you have nothing to show for it? What a waste of your time.

That is the problem with mediocrity. People give up because they don't see instant results and success. This is why it is so important to keep watering your dream and nurturing it because all of a sudden something starts to happen and people stop looking at you in a strange way. They stop laughing and then, they turn to you, and they say, 'I knew it was going to happen, I knew you could do it.' But they never had faith like you did, and your bamboo tree is hitting ninety feet and is now standing strong, tall and proud.

Keep watering and feeding your mind. Knowledge is king in my book because if you're not learning, you're not earning. I have had so many people think I'm crazy, just because I'm focused. I have a goal, I have a vision, and I truly believe in what I'm doing. There is no such thing as a get rich scheme. Sitting on your arse waiting for your lottery results to come in or for some amazing miracle to arise just defeats the purpose. Start creating your future and water that ground over and over and suddenly you will see that first sprout and then I can promise you, you will flourish, and you will grow, standing proud above the crowd and above mediocrity where you deserve to be!

Create Your Own Life.

Life is not about finding yourself; it's about creating yourself. So many of us feel that we have to find ourselves so we can become this extraordinary person, but the truth is you need to start creating who you are and who you want to become. All my life I have always wanted to be this better person because I have a burning desire of wanting the best for myself and all those important people around me. This is where you have to believe in everything you do and work on you, yes YOU!! The only way you are going to create yourself is by developing the areas you need to strengthen.

If you want to be successful then you have to think and act as a successful person does, it's as simple as that. My journey only started when I joined the Entrepreneur Circle because that's when I realised, these are the people I need to surround myself with. There are so many different levels within this community, but every single one of them knows their path that is leading them to create themselves. Life is a choice, and your destination can be where you want it to be: what decisions have you got to make right now this second. To make sure your path is going the right way? I am travelling down a brand new path as I write this and I'm so excited to be able to share my experiences with you. I'm turning into the business owner that I have dreamt of becoming. I'm absolutely buzzing knowing that 2017 is nearly upon us and that means brand new opportunities to grab hold of.

As this year has developed so have I and so have my friends; the support I have had overwhelms me sometimes but knowing I have given back also helps my path as well. Never be afraid to ask for help when creating yourself, because there will always be someone that has travelled down many of the paths you are choosing. Stop doing what is easy and standing around complaining about your situation. Stop doing what is easy and surrendering your dreams and giving up, all that is going to do is make life harder in the long run.

Do the hard stuff now so you can live easier when you get older. You see what I'm saying about creating yourself instead of finding yourself? You can wait an eternity to be happy, so get your arse up and make yourself happy. It may sound repetitive, but it's only because it bloody works and it's true. I'm not giving you a magic formula to your ultimate self; I'm just sharing from the heart what has made me tick. Every day has to be better than yesterday otherwise there is no point in getting up; it's time to start breaking habits that are slowing you down. It's time to let go of people that don't believe in you. It's time to become the person you think about becoming.

It takes sixty-six days to break bad habits, so what's the one thing you can do today, right now that's going to help you move towards creating a better you? Life itself is a test; it just requires desire to push you past every obstacle in your way!

Are you up to the ultimate challenge of being original, being better, being extraordinary? If you have the bounce inside of you, then life is just a piece of cake. I have gone through so much pain in my life just like everybody else, but I'm here bouncing and struggling to sit still as I write this as I can truly say to myself I'm doing everything possible to create a better me.

I don't give up because if I give up then I'm just settling for ordinary and anyone can do that! I will always stay hungry; this is why I look in the mirror every single morning and pull my angry, silly face and say "I'm going to make it". People who are hungry have no excuses because they are unacceptable, losing is not an option because winners win and losers lose! It's as simple as that. Take life by the horns and ride it even if it bucks and kicks. Ride that sucker hard!

Chapter 9

Accountable or Unaccountable?

It's time to make a decision, and it has to be a conscious one! It has to be yours and yours alone. The thing I have learnt over so many years is that you have to be accountable for all of your actions. Everything you do has to have a purpose, you need to know what direction you are travelling in, and on this journey, it does not matter whether you succeed or fail you have to be accountable for every single action. When I say you have to be accountable, you have to take responsibility for all of your actions.

Being unaccountable means you have excuses lining up and excuses are for the weak, the people who are not serious about who, what and where they want to be. Too many people blame their circumstances as to why they are not doing better, too many people blame their upbringing, but life is what you make it. You cannot start dwelling on the past and what could have been because you are living in the now; your decisions and choice start now! There are those that blame the government for how bad they are doing. How does that work? You will also get the people that say someone got lucky. That's my favourite because they do not see the hard work that person has gone through to get to that situation or that stage in their life. All they see is the result. It's all too easy to blame others and the situation, rather than standing up and being counted and taking responsibility for who you are.

Every person in the world will have a story, a chapter in their lives where all was pretty crap, and they had to deal with some rough patches, but that is life. You have to snap out of it and start being accountable.

My childhood was quite normal as my mum always made sure I got awesome Christmas presents and birthday presents. She also made sure we all had a holiday every year, and although it was hard she didn't blame life for throwing her a bad line, she just toughed it out and took responsibility for her actions.

She decided to have all of us kids, and if it meant raising us on her own, she did it. She worked two, three and sometimes four jobs at once to make sure she provided for all of us and made sure the house was looked after. She knew you get out of it what you want most and nothing less.

I can't blame the world because I did not become a professional footballer. I didn't want it bad enough, or I didn't have enough talent, but for years I used to say it's all about who you know and so and so just got lucky. That's a poor excuse. The problem was I didn't train hard enough, I didn't make enough sacrifices, and I didn't follow through on my opportunities. I was young, and I accepted what teachers and peers had told me from a young age when I should have just been following my heart, my passion and my dream. This is why people like Gary Neville and David Beckham inspire me so much. They were not the most gifted footballers in the world when they started; they just had to make themselves accountable for their actions. If they wanted to be professional footballers, they were going to have to get up before everyone in the mornings and stay late after training and practise harder than everyone else. It got them through each and every level with sheer determination and mindset.

Making yourself accountable is a mindset that you have to believe in, just like I did with my self-affirmations and videos. I couldn't be a fraud and say the stuff on my videos and then not do it myself. I had to practise what I was preaching. The amazing thing is that it made me stronger and more determined; I wanted to be that successful person that I talk about all the time.

Another thing to help you be more accountable is to write your goals down with deadlines and share them. You can even have them written down on your bathroom wall so that when friends and family come round, they will see them. If you do that what's the first thing they are going to talk about once they have seen them? Your goals, of course. What does that mean? It means you have to discuss them and explain what they are, why they are there and how close you are from achieving them, making yourself more accountable.

I know that sounds a bit extreme, but if you're not sharing them, you're probably just going to make up a big excuse as to why you're not where you want to be right now because life just got in the way.

Something else to add if you have not got an accountable buddy, then get one, be bold and brave and start making your life one of accountability.

Chapter 10

Rewards

We all work so hard, and if you're reading this book, you are also on a journey to better yourself and learn how to keep that bounce inside of you bouncier than ever. If you are like me, you are aware of how important setting goals must be, if not you are starting to learn the importance of them. Setting goals gives you a destination to head towards, but with every single goal, there should be a reward, something that is satisfactory and compliant with the amount of effort you have put into your goal.

Rewards are important and a massive part of anyone's journey otherwise why are we working so hard? The ultimate aim is to get to a point where we are not working so hard because we put the hard work in now, so our lives become easier.

Many people make this mistake: they try and cut corners now and do the easy stuff first, but by doing this all they do is make their later life so much harder. If you work hard, then you need to make sure your efforts are being rewarded.

If you are setting yourself monthly goals, or quarterly goals the rewards could be a new pair of shoes, a new dress but your twelve-monthly goals could be a new car or a luxury holiday. This way you have always got something to look forward to and get excited about. A reward also has a purpose, because it might not just be you who is getting the reward. It might be your kids, your wife or maybe your whole family but the point is the recognition for your achievements.

A lot of people who know me know that I have worked my little bum off this year and made some massive sacrifices. The reason for this chapter is because without rewards for my achievements I would not be in the place I am now, mentally, physically and in my business. I have mapped out what I wanted to achieve this year and every time I reached a certain milestone I treated either myself, my kids or my wife.

The satisfaction behind all these rewards strives me to set more goals because the more goals I reach, the more and more rewards I get (yes selfish I know, but I love Christmas, and this is what it feels like). I have reached all my monthly goals, and when I did so, the little rewards happen. It's more satisfying than you can imagine getting really expensive shoes or clothes because I felt I deserved them.

If I didn't reach a goal, I simply doubled the reward over to the next one as I then have to complete the next one to receive both. One of my biggest barriers and goals was achieved recently and ahead of schedule so that just meant my reward got pushed forward a few months and here I am still writing parts of my first book on a beach in the Maldives with Linda. Can't be bad, eh?

This rustic island is beautiful, and I could not think of many better places to be, and the greatest part of it is that it was a reward, an awesome reward for working smarter. I do not feel guilty for leaving my business but if honest I am missing Titus (sad face). The point is that I have earned it and so has Linda for bearing with me while I worked so hard. Not only do I get a reward but I get that chance to re-charge my batteries. Equally, I know you have got all sorts of things running through your mind wondering what your rewards could be.

It's necessary that you reward yourself and your family, so create your goals but more importantly attach a reward to them because the reason we work and strive to be better is to work less and provide more.

Chapter 11

No Warranty, No Trade in

Life balance is the key to being positive and productive because we get suckered into all the day to day things that happen around us and forget about ourselves and our families. We all know that life can be hard but if you have a strong enough belief you will understand that working harder and longer hours does not mean more money and more time. The one thing we cannot get back in time, so it's important that we use it wisely to make the most of our lives. What people forget is that we don't have warranties and guarantees like other products in our lives. There is no trade-in option if all of a sudden we burn ourselves to the ground. So be very careful and conscious of what you are doing, why you are doing it and know where you are going.

I took over my business in 2007, and due to many people telling me it was a mistake and I shouldn't have done it, as well as all the people telling me I would fail, I drove myself hard to prove them all wrong. I would work silly hours burn the candle at the other end too, enjoying nights out with my mates thinking I was top of the world. Without realising it, you take your eye off the ball, and then things start to slip. This means you have work even longer hours to get things back on track again and it all takes its toll. Even when you think you are doing really well your body and mind is screaming for a break, and you have to pay attention to this.

Hopefully sharing my story will help you realise what can happen, so you can avoid the mistakes I made or learn from them. I know many people who have been in my position, and it is important that you have people around you for support and who believe in what you are doing. However, it's also about learning to work smarter and be smarter with your time.

Four years ago I had my first breakdown. I had never experienced anything like that before. Anyone who knows me knows how bouncy I am and I'm a bundle of fun, loving life. I love to smile, laugh and make sure everyone is on that journey with me. When I finally burnt myself out, I fell so hard from so high up. When it happened, I was bloody scared. My body just shut down on me, but even then my brain was telling me to stop being so silly. My warranty was up, and I needed a new one.

I'm a very strong-willed person, so I knew I would overcome it, but it also came down to the amazing people I have around me and the belief I have in where I was going. It took some serious conversations with people explaining to me that it is time to start working smarter. This is when you have to sit up and take notice and figure out that you need to rest and you can't just keep working and working; you need time to yourself.

If you want your life to move forward and you want that bounce in your life to continue bouncing, planning your future is the only way to do it.

As well as planning your business goals it is also important to plan your family time and free time at the beginning of every year so that you, your family and your work, know exactly when you will be having your time-outs.

This has been a major part of my success as I plan out every weekend I'm spending with my boys going to watch Manchester United play football and also getting that quality father-son time. It also lets my wife know when we are going on holiday, so when I'm working crazy hard, there is always an end goal and a result. Also, the people in my business knows that nothing can be put in during these times. This creates work-life balance, and everyone I know that is doing this is achieving super success, personally and in business.

Keep making the steps in getting the balance right. If your warranty does run out, there is no guarantee what the outcome could be. Think smart, work smart and never lose your bounce.

Chapter 12

Unlocking your potential

When we are children, we are able to express ourselves however, and whenever we please, this enables us to unlock our true potential. What I mean by this is that we are all learning new skills and developing as a human being. We are totally and wholeheartedly encouraged to move forward and believe in achieving our next goals.

Take walking for example. Our parents encourage us to stand up, put that foot in front of the other and make that next step and if we fall down the next encouragement comes to get back up off our backside and start again. We do not accept failure as an option, and the power, determination and the opportunity to discover new things takes control. We are unlocking our potential from such an early age. As the years go by we still push to learn new things and explore which in turn teaches us to dream! Then senior school begins, and for some, it's easier than it is for others, as this is where some get told they have to hold back. This is where our power gets restricted because if you do not fit into someone's regime or system, you get told you are not allowed to dream.

Don't Be A Goose

Somewhere in us all is the potential to be amazing, to be awesome and take on challenges that we didn't think were possible. Finding out about yourself and understanding that there is so much more to life than our current situation is mind-blowing. Too many people get caught up in their current affairs and believe that is it for them, and that life cannot get any better. I'm here to tell you that is bullshit!

If you want something out of life, you have to earn it. You have to want something bad enough that you know that for change to happen, you have to change your life. To unlock your true potential, sacrifices have to be made. They may only be small to start with, but small daily improvements are the key to long-term results. If you can change your mind, you can change your attitude, and if you can make those changes, you will change your situation and unlock your potential.

It all comes down to you and what you think you're worth? Only you have the power to unlock what truly needs to be released. There is no such thing as "can't" or "I will do it tomorrow" because tomorrow never comes. This is about taking action and taking it now. It's time to start getting your ideas written down imagining your life the way you want it to be. If you can imagine it, then you can achieve it.

I never said unlocking your potential would be easy, but that's what makes it a journey; believing in yourself and knowing the idea of being successful is achievable.

The saying I use for this now is "Be More Wasp." I know some of you think wasps are the most useless and annoying insect in the world but a wasp never gives up in his challenge. When you have that sweet sugary drink or food on your table, and wasp just keeps coming for you, what do you do? You swat him away, but back he comes over and over and over again! Why? Because he is persistent and he wants a taste and is making it his mission to get some. That's a trait I have, and I know you do too, so start unlocking it and using it! "Be More Wasp."

Learning is the key to unlocking your potential because the more knowledge you have, the more confident you become. I have spent years studying and learning, and this facility is there for you too. It could come from the internet, from friends or even going back to school to study. In a world full of information it is down to you to find your wisdom.

Unlock your potential and see how big the world really is. I hope you are starting to feel that fire in your belly because I'm getting excited for you. Let's open new doors together and show the world what true potential looks like. Naysayers and haters can keep being mediocre while we create and determine what our future holds instead of letting someone else do it for us!!

Chapter 13

Becoming the owner

Understanding your journey makes everything worthwhile and keeps the bounce inside of you alive, so you have to ask yourself what keeps you bouncing and how high do you want to go?

For years I felt like I was a manager even though I owned my own business and this is the case for many others, but you need to realise the truth if you are going to make something of yourself. I talk about how key knowledge is but knowledge is nothing without action, and this was my powerful lesson in learning to become a business owner. Here are some of my key learnings from the journey:

The mind shift
1   realising trading time for money, does not create success.
2   working on your business, not in it.
3   leading your team, not managing them.
4   being semi-retired
5   being aware of complacency
6   having systems in the right places

The mindset
1   others can run my business for me

2   wealth has nothing to do with time
3   always working smarter, not harder
4   understanding of a passive income
5   how important it is to trust people
6   seeking new opportunities

As you make the switch from being a manager to becoming an owner the bounce in you gets stronger and stronger. You have to take control of yourself and your beliefs and reduce the distractions in your life. My biggest strength is self-affirmations because whatever your telling yourself about yourself becomes a controlling thought.

If you were to look at amazing tennis players like Andy Murray, do you think he takes ownership of himself before every game of tennis he plays? What do you think he is saying to himself before he steps out onto that court to face his challenger? He will be saying that he is going to win, that he is going to destroy whoever gets in his way, no one can stop him, and the trophy will be his no matter what!

Becoming the business owner is about taking control of yourself, your self-belief system and owning your subconscious. Self-affirmations work for me as they do for so many other top business owners and professional sports stars. Don't let setbacks and obstacles get in the way of you reaching your goals and become the owner of every aspect of your life.

When you start to take ownership of something you start to feel the power surge through your body; you feel that buzzing and understanding of why you are doing what you are doing. This then turns into laser focus, stops procrastination and increases performance. Becoming an owner creates accountability and makes you responsible for every action you take. Are you sitting there reading and questioning what needs to change in your life, what actions do you need to take to move your ship into the line of the wind so that you can set your sails and feel the force of the wind?

Becoming an owner takes hard work and courage as you realise your weaknesses, admitting you're not doing enough and things have to change. Don't be scared though, my biggest fear was not knowing my numbers well enough and was scared to admit this. However, after my business coach gave me a wakeup call, I knew I had to take control of this area as well. Which is exactly what I did and now I have that control.

Becoming an owner can mean so many different things to different people as everyone is on their own journey, but once you take ownership of yourself and understand a little bit more about your purpose, you can become the owner of your destination and destiny.

Chapter 14

Why are you doing this?

Many people don't even know why they are doing what they are doing; they are just following the motions of something that they thought was right. This happens because we are guided by what we are told or shown. We never truly understand the true concept of why? You need to appreciate the end goal and why you are doing what you are doing and the only way to do this is to understand its purpose.

Let me tell you a story that I was told about a roast turkey.

One Christmas evening while sitting down for dinner a young woman asks her husband why he chops the legs off the turkey before cooking it. His reply was, 'I'm not really sure, it's how my mum always did it.'

The following year, they went to his mum's house for Christmas dinner and out of curiosity, remembering his wife's question from last year's Christmas dinner, he asks his mum why she chops the legs off the turkey while cooking it. She turns and says 'If I'm totally honest I don't actually know, it's something Nan used to do so I have always done it.' Later that evening Nan visited the house, and everyone was curious now about the turkey cooking process. So curiously they ask Nan, 'Why do you chop off the legs while cooking the turkey?' With a quick response, she says 'Because it sat better on the baking tray.'

We just follow a trend or a situation because we have always seen things done that way but not actually known why. What a waste of turkey for so many years!

Don't be a goose and always follow the flock just because that's what they do. Think about your end goal, and by knowing this, you figure why you want it so bad.

I was out for dinner with my whole family one evening enjoying a lovely Chinese dinner, when I got chatting to my little sister Kayleigh. She seemed disheartened about something, so I asked her what was wrong. She begins to tell me that she is worried about her weight and appearance because she is going away in eight weeks' time. She tells me she is just stopping eating as that seems like the best thing to do, but we all know that's not the best way at all, it's probably the worst. This all comes down to a little education and guidance. I explain to her what she should do, but she still sees this as hard work and doesn't believe she will get to where she wants to be in the desired timescale.

I made a quick phone call to my man Aaron Philips from Fitstart UK and explained the situation my amazing little sister is in. By the next day, he has had a phone conversation with her and invited her down to his gym for a consultation. Later that day my phone rings, and it's Kayleigh, and she begins to moan and moan about her weight again. Her exact words were 'No wonder I'm fat. It costs so much money to be fit!' You can imagine how hard I laughed, bless her. I sat up and got her to explain why. She told me that for Aaron to get her in the shape she needs to be in for her holiday, she has got to train four days a week, be put on a very strict diet and it's going to cost £600. She also says 'Oh you'll never guess what? He wants the money up front!' she shouts. I continue to laugh, but in a nice way, of course.

I reply, 'So let's get this right Kayleigh, you want to have the perfect beach body for your holiday in eight weeks' time, correct?'

'Yes,' she replies.

'Ok,' I say 'So let's look at it like this, so what if I said to you, give me £600 now, and tomorrow I promise you your beach body, what would you say to that?'

She replies very quickly and sharply, 'No worries, I will get the cash for you now.'

'Right so there is the first obstacle, removed the money. So let's now break it down even further. Are you willing to train four days a week for eight weeks

if you got the perfect beach body and it cost you nothing?'
Another very quick reply, 'Yes, easy peasy.'

I reply with 'So there is another obstacle removed.'
Kayleigh is starting to see the bigger picture now and also understanding why she is doing this in the first place.
I explain to her what her goal is through a little education and she starts to get a bit excited. So I now do one final breakdown, ''So Aaron wants £600 over eight weeks? That's £75 a week, which is roughly £11 a day! Are you telling me to achieve your desired goal you are not willing to spend £11 a day?'
The phone went silent for a couple of seconds, and an excited laugh and response came back, 'Yeah, of course, I am, I didn't look at it like that before,' she says.
I explain that too many people get caught up with the big picture too many times instead of breaking it down into bite-size chunks and understanding how easy something really can be, especially if you want it bad enough.
She said 'I'm going now and I'm ringing Aaron right away.'
Now you don't all have to guess, but yes my beautiful and gorgeous little sister got the desired result in the eight weeks she set herself and she looked awesome and had the most amazing holiday because of it. She understood what and why she was working so damn hard, and she got her rewards at the end of it too.

Was it hard work? Of course it bloody was! Was it worth it? Damn, right it was! I don't think I have seen my sister so bouncy. She had worked her little arse off to get something she truly wanted, and it felt good because it was all her own doing. There was blood, sweat and tears along the way but the most important thing here is that she knew why she was doing it and that motivated her and pushed her to the end.

What I like about this story is that it is something so small that just needs to be broken down for us to understand what is important to us and why we do things to make them happen. Also, I got to watch my little sister accomplish something awesome, listening to her story as she went through the eight weeks was amazing because I knew what she was going through and what the pain must have felt like. But I also know how great that feeling is when your mind shifts and nothing gets in the way of your goals.

Always understand properly why you are doing what you are doing and don't let the size or cost of something deter you. Break it down into sizeable chunks that are comfortable enough for you to work with and never lose sight of the long-term goal. There is never a quick fix for anything so stay focused and educate yourself for what is needed to make every step possible.

Chapter 15

Butchers or dieticians?

It's important to understand about options and opportunities around you because the more options available, the more doors that you can unlock and when you unlock new doors, your bounce gets stronger as you start to unravel the greatness inside of you.

Throughout my lifetime it's always been so crucial that I'm always enhancing my development and learning all the time. At every level I have been at, knowing what is needed to create a better environment has been key to all the successes I have in life. As you read earlier when I was the warehouse boy wanting to get on the shop floor to sell, I had to learn; I had to adapt to new surroundings to make myself better. I did not accept that being in the warehouse was what I was destined for; decisions had to be made. Every day in our lives we have choices to make, and we can choose to be a butcher, or we can choose to be a dietician. You see by making the right choices to suit your life or, even better, to create the life you want, you have to make sure that you're not restricting yourself to what is put in front of you. Many people I know struggle to see what's around them because they have their negative blinkers on, they have been so discouraged about making changes that they refuse to see how wide they could open their eyes.

The reason why I'm so bouncy all the time is that my eyes light up at the prospect of a new opportunity and that's exactly how I see every new day. There is always something that can make your life better and new ways to achieve your goals and your dreams.

Let's take this year for example, although it was extremely tough without the challenges I would not have broken through my barriers. I had to constantly be on the lookout for ways to develop myself, my business and my lifestyle. Keeping in touch with the latest trends and staying consistent with my actions has been a key element. Could you imagine if gave up after a few weeks because it was tough and hard work? That was not an option if my dreams were going to be achieved; I needed to make sure I was feeding myself with all the right ingredients and also had to be prepared to let go of all the juicy distractions that could quite easily deter me from the end result.

This is my point with the butcher or the dietician. If you walk into a butchers shop, you know what you are going to get. It will be some juicy, delicious, succulent meat that just makes your mouth water. There is nothing wrong with that, and I'm the first to admit that you can't beat a good steak, but you are getting only one food option, meat! When you ask a dietician for some food or a food plan, it is constantly changing. The dietician realises that there is always going to be a better product to enhance your every choice and that choice that will fulfil your end result. Being the dietician, you're always on the lookout for a better way to reach your goals, and you're not confined to just meat. Variety and options are what make you a better person; it's what makes the bounce keep on bouncing.

This works with your surroundings as well. If you're stuck around the same people who don't have ambition, then you're not seeing what other people are doing to make their lives better. As in why the successful are successful. Opening your horizons can only be a good thing!

Start exploring what else there is available for you, don't be shy and most certainly don't let anyone stand in your way of great opportunities. Make the change, and if necessary make the sacrifices and become the dietician in your life.

Adam's story.

About a month ago I got a phone call from Adam, and he asked if we could go out and grab something to eat. I had some time, so after settling on a lovely sushi restaurant, Adam picked me up. Once we arrived at the restaurant Adam let rip and started to tell me that he has had enough, he is lost and feels he can no longer continue running his own business. I was stunned as this is a man who is just as bouncy as me and full of life. To hear this from him took me aback a little. I asked him to slow down and explain what was going on, what had happened to suddenly have this change of heart.

Adam started to let me know that he had fallen quite badly in debt and that his staff relationships had broken down and in turn, this was causing no end of trouble for him and his clients. Surprisingly he was still extremely busy, so that wasn't the problem. We began to talk about the ins and outs of his business and how to get this turned around. The question I had to ask him was, did he still want his business and was his heart still in it?

It was a tough question for him because things had got so bad in his head he was already making plans to go work for someone else. However, after getting down to the nitty-gritty, he didn't want what he had spent the last four years building up just to disappear from underneath him. This was a good sign.

For the next hour, we talked about getting rid of dead wood within the business, demoting staff members, understanding what his company's core values were, timekeeping and time management, business systems and processes and finally, money.

I explained to him that it was all his fault and that the only person he can blame was himself. With a massive smile now on his face, he understood where I was coming from and started to excitingly talk about what he was going to do to get these actions started. This was when I started to get excited as well, because everything that I had learnt over the years from real life experiences, books and seminars I had attended, was all coming into great use. I was passing on some of the knowledge to make sure Adam's business would thrive.

After some very tasty sushi and plenty of water, Adam and I called it a night. We were both buzzing with enthusiasm on the journey home; a total transformation from the journey out. As we said our goodbyes, I told him I would be calling him over the next few days before I jetted off to the Maldives to see how he was getting on. I was as good as my word, and I made the call so Adam was well prepared for what was ahead of him. I left him to it as I was looking forward to my holiday with Linda.

After an amazing holiday, I arrive back home in wet and rainy England buzzing like crazy after my rest and reading three books. My phone had been off for a week, but as I get home and get comfortable the phone goes on and it goes crazy, but I was secretly looking forward to it. I look at my messages, and I have a few from Adam; I'm so keen to look at them. To my astonishment, one of them says, 'Gary, you saved my business, and I love you!' That was the best welcome home present ever and gave me the biggest smile. I had to phone him up straight away to find out what had happened and what he had done to turn things around in just over a week?

Just hearing his voice you could hear the excitement and the belief in him. I ask 'What did you do?']

His quick response is 'I just took action Gary like you said.' He continued, 'I put some small systems in place at the workshop and made sure that the rules where followed. I had a chat with the staff and explained what was going on and where we needed to be. I put some laws in place to re-affirm the control, but the biggest thing I did Gary, was that I took control of my life. I understood that it was all my fault and if my situation was going to change then, I had to change it. I got myself in that position, so it is my responsibility to get myself out of it.'

You can't even imagine how powerful that sounded to me. I loved his enthusiasm; he said it wasn't easy and he had to make some really tough decisions and have some serious conversations with people.

Although I was grateful to hear his happiness I had to explain that it was he that had saved the business and not me. He was the one that took action and knew what was needed; he was the one who put in the graft and the thinking time to make it happen.

If you are like my friend Adam, you have to stand up and be counted and take control of your life. There is no room for excuses and poor performances. You either want to achieve your dreams or you don't. As I say, "you are responsible for making your dreams a reality" and Adam is living proof of that.

Chapter 16

Don't fear talent

I learnt a valuable lesson while I was at school and that was not to fear talent. What do I mean by this? Teachers have a funny way of helping kids develop as it seems they only look for the most academically talented kids. If a child has a natural ability at something, they are very good at giving them the attention and the time rather than focusing on the kids that have hidden determination. From a very early age I had to discover that if I wanted something bad enough, or if I wanted to be good at something, I simply had to work my arse off to achieve it. I think that is an important lesson for anyone; just because someone appears to be better than you at something does not mean they will continue to be better! Having a hard work ethic out-weighs any talent you can have. Being determined to succeed, having the desire to push yourself to new heights, now that is the best talent of all.

Not being chosen by my school football team was probably my first experience of learning that you should not fear talent. It instilled a driver in me that stays with me to this day; I made it my mission to work harder and train harder than all of those kids that were more talented than me. I'm not going to sit here and say I turned into the most amazing footballer because I didn't, but I became very good, and there wasn't one person that put more effort in than me. I ate, slept, drank and lived for football. I watched the best footballers and had a fire in my belly that I could play for the team and I would prove people wrong those that judged me. I'm sure many of you have had this experience, and this continues to drive me on and keep my bounciness alive.

Never give up just because someone is more talented than you. Every challenge I have overcome has been the product of wanting it more than my competitor, whether this is in sport or business. My business challenges have been the greatest of all. How does a small independent bathroom and kitchen company stand out in the crowd of so many big national brands? I tell you how. It is through learning; knowledge is king but only if you take consistent action and use that knowledge to its best ability.

I go on every course that is going to develop a skill that will enhance my reputation. I read books that will enhance my abilities; I study the things that I don't know much about, I put my money where my mouth is and invest in things that will help my business grow. Not knowing something encourages me to learn more and to learn as much about it as I can.

Talent is a word that gets touted around too much, but even the most talented people understand that they will not stay the best without effort, passion, desire and determination. They understand that there will always be someone who will want to take their place at the helm. If the most successful sports people, movie stars, musicians and entrepreneurs understand that talent is not enough, it's time we understood it as well.

We have the ultimate power in deciding who and what we want to be; not our teachers, not our friends, not our peers and especially not our families. What decision will you make when you have an idea you want to pursue or an urge you want to fulfil? You might not be talented in this area right now, but if you want it bad enough, you will become so if you are willing to fight for it and work for it.

Never fear talent and embrace the fact that you have much to learn. All you have to do then is work bloody hard for it.

Inspiration

As I continue to share my story, the more I start to understand more about our purpose. For many years I have been trying to figure what is my purpose and why I'm doing what I'm doing. My original belief was to be a great bathroom designer, to be the best I could and see where that took me. Why was my thinking like that? The only reason I can think of was that of all the times that I was told I wouldn't accomplish anything in my life. That meant that my purpose has been to prove so many people wrong and show the world that I am somebody. I have become so good at designing bathrooms and running my business that I thought that is who I was! My passion is bathrooms because I'm good at it! But it's only over the last few weeks that I'm discovering that my purpose is to help others.

If I use my idea of bathrooms first, this might make more sense. I get so much satisfaction from going to a client's house and talking to them about their grotty old bathroom and how we can make it a sanctuary for them to enjoy. I get excited knowing that I can be creative and start inspiring them by showing them what the possibilities are. By the time I leave their home, they feel as excited as I do and can't wait to receive my designs.

Once I get to my studio and start working on their design, this is where my imagination gets to work, and I am creative. Once they have seen the designs, they are as excited as me. I have made a dramatic, positive change in their lives and something they can enjoy for many years. The really big impact for me is not the money, it's the satisfaction of making someone smile and being a part of their life, even if it is just for a short while. Money is the by-product whereas inspiration and positive change is the real reason I do it.

Discovering this purpose really came to light when an amazing friend, Ash Taylor, pointed this out this to me. Ash said to me, 'bathrooms have only been a part of your journey, and may continue to be so, but giving back and being driven means you have more strings to your bow than you first realised.'

He continued to say that because of all the things I'm doing with my videos and all the hard work spent developing my skill base it can only benefit the world in another way. These were powerful words and hearing them from Ash meant even more because of the respect that I have for him.

It doesn't matter what you are doing at this moment I can assure you at some point you are making a positive change in someone else's life. When your passion is at 100% and your potential is at 100% your purpose comes into alignment and with that comes inspiration, true inspiration. The smallest gesture you can make could turn out to be a life changer in someone else's world.

Inspiration travels in circles. The reason we get inspired is because we want to achieve greatness, we want to be the best person we can be, and we want to succeed. The reason we do this is so that we can inspire others. Think about your true purpose. Mine is to put as much bounce in as many people's lives as I can. Your job to inspire every person you can to make something of their lives, to be the creator of their destiny.

Don't be a wheel clamper, instead, make a positive change in people's lives and remember that inspiration travels in circles. Start your circle and watch the powerful impact you create.

Chapter 17

Stop complaining about life

Don't you get fed up of people complaining about their circumstances and how life has been so cruel to them? Always saying that people are lucky they are successful and rich! This really gets my goat as those are the people are not willing to change their environment to make a positive change in their lives. The same people that will make that New Year's Resolution on the 31st of December and say this year is going to be my best year ever, things are going to be awesome yet knowing full well they are not going to do anything that will change their lives. How can you believe that your life is going to get better if you don't make the right sacrifices and have a positive outlook on life?

The reason for my little rant is that life can be shit, it will throw all sorts of crap at you and your family, but it's how you react to it that makes you a success. You are always going to get hit, you are always going to get knock backs that throw you to the ground, and this is where you need that bounce, that positive notion that no matter what happens you will fight back.

We all used to play conkers at school, didn't we? And what was the purpose of your awesome conker? It was to take as many hits as it could and then smash through the other person's conker. If that happened then you would be crowned conker champion! And that is all life is; you have to toughen up and be resilient to hard times. You're not here to crack; you're here to understand your purpose which is to make a positive change in yours and someone else's life. Understand that you have passion and desire so deeply ingrained into you that you're not going take anything lying down, you get to make the choices that change your life no matter how bad things are today, having a positive outlook on everything truly inspires you to move forward with your life.

This part of my book has been inspired by such an amazing boy, a boy that is just a superstar and an inspiration to me, my family and so many other people around him and that boy is my little nine-year-old cousin Ossie Robinson.

Ossie has Neuroblastoma Cancer and has been fighting this for two and a half years now. He has recently just had to have whole body radiation as well as a stem cell transplant. He was at stage three cancer but has now moved up to stage four. He currently has eight cancerous tumours in his body and is about to spend the next six weeks going through very high doses of chemotherapy. However, this is an amazing boy because no matter what life

124

has thrown at him, he doesn't stop smiling. He keeps fighting because he has a goal, he has a dream, and that is to be a footballer. This boy has an amazing talent on the football pitch and up until the age of seven when he got diagnosed he was high up on Arsenal and Watford's list of talents to watch. Even now Ossie still has that belief inside of him that pushes him, that desire to follow what is his own goal and why not? Why should he not have that belief in himself?

Another thing he strives for is his awesome hairstyles; he loves having all sorts of haircuts and patterns shaved into his head, having the chance to gel his hair and create the style of his choice! He is a true inspiration; you just can't do anything but admire him and, of course, cuddle him every time you see him.

When I see him, I reflect and understand that my life is a piece of cake compared to his and this is one of the reasons why I have so much bounce inside of me. Nothing is restricting me from achieving my goals, and the only person that can stop me is myself! When you have something as powerful as that to reflect on, nothing else compares. Look at me when I was crying on my shop floor complaining about my circumstances! How pathetic was I? What a cry baby! This is why I shook myself down and got on with things. This is where reality kicked in, and I realised my situation could be so much worse, and it's time to be bloody grateful.

Obviously, Ossie's Mum and Dad have struggled with this situation as any parents would, but they should be given awards for how strong they have been. It must hurt so much inside, but when you have a son who smiles through all the hard times, it helps everyone to stay strong. They are amazing characters that I truly love with all my heart, they are not taking it lying down, and they keep on fighting.

If you have loved ones who are going through this, I'm with you and share my total love but never give up! I don't care what a doctor says to you; it's your positive attitude that shines brighter than anything else. Surround yourself with the right people and make your environment the one you deserve. Take stock of where you are and what you needed to get things done.

Don't be a complainer, be a winner. If you have to fight then fight, but stay positive no matter what. Failure is part of success, and everyone has to go through it. There are hundreds of Ossie's out there battling every day and if they can battle then so can you.

Gut wrenching pain

I went out for dinner with two of my best and closest

friends, Chris and Alan, and we got onto the subject of positive outcomes from tough life situations. These two have known me since I was five years old as we all grew up on the same street and have pretty much done everything together. After discussing these situations that we have had to go through to get where we are today, they both turned to me and told me they salute me for always being so positive in life and dealing with bad situations. At first, I was taken aback and asked what you mean?

Chris began to talk about how most people's objective in life is to make sure they get to spend as much time with their kids as they possibly can and as we know that is tough getting the work and family balance right. The one thing I have had to do all my life is to make the most of every single second with my two boys as they do not live with me and have not done so from very young ages. I have two boys from two separate relationships, and both ended when my boys were two years old (an unfortunate coincidence).

What Chris and Alan were referring to was my never say die attitude because unfortunately, I had to fight two court cases to see my boys on a regular basis. I knew there was a battle on my hands, but for now, this was the ultimate pain as I went from seeing my boys three days a week every week to not seeing them at all and it broke my heart.

The fear of not having regular access to my kids severely damaged me, but there was no way I was going to let that happen, I would rather die than let them take my boys away from me. I set out to make sure this did not happen. I stayed positive throughout and stuck to my version of the truth. I was convinced that someone would listen.

The court case went on for months but I stood my corner and luckily I had true people around me supporting me all the way, and I stayed positive. When the final day came, and I sat there in front of the judges for their verdict. I was as nervous as hell, and when the judges ruled that I could see my boys every Sunday only between 12-3pm, I fell to the floor. I collapsed with disbelief and could barely breathe and the tears rolled down my face; I ran out of the court with the sickest feeling in my belly. It was gut-wrenching. After about half an hour though I had to make my way back up the stairs and as I sat there distraught all of a sudden her solicitor turned and said that they have decided to not go ahead with all of this and access can continue as normal!

I couldn't believe it! The anger boiled up inside me, but at the same time I had the joy of knowing I could see my boys without restrictions. It was confusing, but at least the right result (for the boys and me) came out in the end.

People can keep knocking us back as much as they want but they will never be able to take our desire, our passion and self-belief away because that is ours to stay so that we can make the choices in life that make our future better. Challenges are put in front of us for a reason, and that is to see us overcome them. I'm sure Chris and Alan felt the pain I was going through as they are parents themselves. Because I have friends like them, I can continue to fight any fight that ever gets put in front of me.

Chapter 18

I believe in something bigger than myself

It's funny how life changes as you learn to change yourself. The last year has been amazing for me in so many ways, but you do truly discover who you are as you develop yourself and your skills. I have put in so much effort this year deciphering where I need to be and where I am going, but I truly believe that I'm destined for something bigger than myself. This may sound like a crazy thing to say, but I have been overwhelmed the support from great friends, and it has put a lot of things into perspective.

As I got deeper and deeper with my Gazza Bounce videos, things have changed for the better, and the reactions I was getting from people inspired me even more. It brings so much joy to my heart knowing how powerful a positive attitude can be and how bringing a bit of bounce into everyone's morning can change the outcome of their day. I created Gazza Bounce to help myself get motivated and to make myself accountable, but would never have thought that I would impact other people the way I have.

People have started to connect with me and understand why you need to be so bouncy in life if you are going to achieve your goals and dreams. It is like an infectious smile. So many people are contacting me saying how much they appreciate everything I'm doing and saying in my videos and that it keeps impacting their own life choices! Imagine that? Impacting people's life choices!!

People have told me that they went for their ideal job because I said if you're unhappy in what you do, stop doing it and change it. I have had someone tell me they went to Australia because I give them the confidence to quit their job and pursue a dream. You can imagine how this is all blowing my mind, the former sixteen-year-old bathroom warehouse boy, inspiring people! This has completely changed my outlook on life and where I'm going, but more importantly, it's made me realise that I'm destined for something bigger than myself and that helping others and making a positive change in others' lives can be achieved.

I have always believed in myself and now I feel that even more profoundly. Sharing is caring in my eyes and my energy and enthusiasm for life needs to be shared with the world.

Why did I write this book? I decided to go on a book writing course to write a book about bathroom design and sales, but as I arrived a few people that I have never met before come up to me and say, 'Wow Gary it's so great to finally meet you. I have been watching your videos every day, and they have helped me bounce out of bed and get my life back on track.' I was taken aback by this and didn't know what to think. This was followed up by man teaching the class, Damian, telling me that I should get my positive energy on paper and share that instead! Not knowing what to say I acknowledged it and decided to write this book instead.

While at the awards ceremony I was talking about earlier I get chatting to some people that inspire me when one of them says that I inspire them! I can't believe what I'm hearing once again; I'm inspiring someone that I look up to! He said to me that he always watches my videos and looks forward to them showing up in his Facebook feed every day. I was shocked, but pleased as well.

Giving out this daily energy means I get a massive response from all sorts of people from all walks of life and it gives me so much pleasure to be helping in any way I can.

One of my goals is to tell a little bit about my own story to younger people or even people on a journey of their own. I want everyone to know that it doesn't matter what age you are or what your dreams are, they can be achieved. Since I have been doing this, I have been asked to speak in front of thirty kids for London village, and that's when it hit home for me. I get to talk to kids about my journey and my background. Many of them related to the fact you can succeed and be positive about life if you're willing to believe in yourself and not let others deter you from your path. If you truly care about what you are doing, as long as you practise hard enough then anything is possible.

As I to wrote this book I understand more and more about my destiny. It's in my heart that everyone deserves to release a deep power of desire that is inside of them. If I can help get that released, I feel that is my calling. I wish as I was growing up I knew about this information. I wish it were as easy to find as it is now, but it is what it is.

People should never do what makes them unhappy, what is the point of working hard at something you don't enjoy? You will get the people saying it's to make ends meet but you can make ends meet doing what you enjoy if you believe in yourself. It's attitude that is everything.

How about now?

Now is always the best time to start something new, or taking steps to move forward. Right now is easily the best time to create new goals or develop skills and understanding that will be of benefit in the long term.

If you are wondering when the best time to start a period of personal development, then how about now? Why wait until tomorrow to make positive changes in your life when you can start now? Far too many people have wasted opportunities to do something with their life and life can run away from you without you realising. There are 86,400 seconds in every day. Can you imagine how much better your life will be if you try to maximise as many of these seconds you can every day?

You don't want to look back on life and feel as though you missed your chances. If you are committed to making changes, you can set yourself a goal of five years and then look back on what has occurred in that time. If you are serious about making improvements and living a better life, it is important for you to be positive and make changes right now.

If you don't make changes, you'll be living the same life further down the line, and you'll question yourself once again. There are genuine opportunities to move forward in life, but you need to take action. How about now?

George Croft and the trust of a partner

George has been an important part of my journey,

and this is where I thank him for just being himself. Trust is a massive part of any journey, and that is exactly what George has done throughout this long path we have taken together so far. I have opened my wings and seen how far I can fly, and it's because I have had such a good friend in George to allow me to do so. While in business with George I got to make a lot of decisions because of his trust. I have developed every part of my business with the strength of George behind me. I may have taken the reins of the business but I have always had George to lean on, and for that, I am truly grateful. George has encouraged me to do what's right or even what I thought was right and that's the difference.

Every challenge I have faced and wanted to overcome, George accepted everything as a positive. Because of trust and the relationship we have built, I have turned into the ambitious business owner that I am today. When you have a relationship like that you start to understand what you can achieve from life. So this is a massive thank you to the best business partner I could have ever asked for on my journey to finding out my own personal WHY?

Chapter 19

Mum

So why a chapter about my mum? We didn't have much when we were growing up, but the one thing I never went without was love and encouragement. My mum worked at least three jobs all her life and made sure me, my brother and my two sisters had most things in life. She couldn't afford many of the material things we craved as kids throughout the year, but come Christmas mornings and birthdays we always did just fine. Those mornings were always the best, and the presents under the tree were always endless for us all, and I cannot remember a time I didn't get what I wanted. Except for two years running when I begged Santa for a drum kit which never arrived!

This is to say thank you to my mum for working her arse off while we were all so young, showing the most amazing courage, determination, desire and passion to make sure our home was always perfect and that we always got the things that other kids had. We were my mum's life, and she let everybody know as much. She is a very proud woman, and she has instilled in me that desire to succeed and to never give up. I will keep pursuing my dreams because I want to repay my mum's belief in me. So thank you, mum, for being there when you were always needed the most and thank you for just being you and showing me the true meaning of persistence.

Nigel Botterill.

I was recently at an EC national event with many people in the room listening to Kris Akabusi who was talking on stage. He talked about a mentor of his from a very young age, who believed in him and had faith that he could achieve great things when he had no faith in himself. This mentor was called Sergeant McKenzie. This got me thinking about how important it is to have someone like this in all of our lives, to look up to, to respect and take faith that we can all be great if we have the right mentor and guidance.

Who was this person was in my life and I always believed that I never had this person, but then I looked around and realised where I was and why my personal and business life is the way it is. Nigel Botterill! If I had not been introduced to Nigel and had the opportunity to see him in action helping so many people in so many different ways, my business and even my marriage, might not be in the state it is in now.

Nigel created inspiration for me; he showed me that anything is possible if you want it bad enough and that anyone can have success. Nigel's pure energy and determination were there for all to see and that's when I latched on and saw my future. I saw the possibilities for my family and me. Nigel created a platform for like-minded people to be in the same room and share experiences, to engage with one another, supporting each other and building true friendships. I have been inspired by Nigel for the last six years of my life and still get excited about what he is going to bring to the table next. When I am in the same room with him, at dinner or watching him on stage, I just know something amazing is going to happen in my life because we are talking about a man who has a track record of success. His passion, desire and commitment never falter and that is why he is my own personal Sergeant McKenzie, the man who has made everything possible for me to achieve the success I am having right now.

It is important to find this person, as I did, in your life. It could be your mum, dad, a teacher, a friend but you need to make sure you have the right person to look up to and inspire you. To teach you that anything is possible if your purpose is meaningful and strong enough for you to commit to.

Thank you, Nigel, for being an inspiration to me, and so many others, but for also being a straight talker and making clear that it was me that needed to achieve success and bring the best out of my character.

Obsession is the key that will unlock any door you choose to open.

Obsession is a massive part of any dream or goal you are chasing, and it's what has kept me bouncing year after year. If you crave something and you want it bad enough, you will go after it. There have been many times in this book that I have talked about the challenges that you and I all face.

Obsession used and channelled correctly can unlock any doors. I sit here writing this obsessing about what my future holds for me knowing that only I get to make that a reality. I look at my vision board; I look at my goals and dreams that sit in front of me and obsess about what it is going to take to make that happen. I obsess about finishing this book and adding this to my list of things that I have managed to achieve. If my book gets through to one person and changes their life for the better that's all that matters. This has been my obsession for the last five months, and it's been one of the most amazing and uplifting experiences of my life. This is starting to feel very heartfelt, but that's because I believe in every single word that I have written and it has all come from my heart and soul.

I feel myself repeating words I have already said. A different result requires you doing something differently, so what is the one thing that you are going to change, and do today, that will shape the rest of your life?

Never be governed by any upbringing or life situation because results change if you are brave enough and dare to stand up and not accept no as the final answer to your dreams. Without this obsession, I have no bounce to continue and no one will ever stop me from having a life full of bounce.

Chapter 20

#GazzaBounce

All of these are transcripts from the 'Don't Be A Goose' videos that I've been putting out on YouTube and social media. Each one has a message, and they are all exactly as I said them on the day.

One:

'Dreams mean you need to make sacrifices in life! All you have to do is create a habit and by creating a habit you create change and change mean you have finally stepped out of your comfort zone. If you keep doing the same things every day, you achieve the same things! Is that what you really want? So be brave, make the change and turn your dream into a reality.

Something you have to realise is that you don't have to be great to get started, but you have to get started to be great! So think about that today and realise anything is possible if you are willing to put in the work!

Don't wish life was easier, wish you were better. Too many people are scared of hard work, but you need to realise if it were easy everyone would be successful. So don't wait for tomorrow or the perfect time as there will never be that time just the same old excuses you make up every day. Opportunities are missed every day because they are dressed up in overalls, and it looks like work! Make the change.

Let's talk about risks as in life you have to take some to achieve greatness in life. Let's face it if you win; you will be so happy: if you lose all that has to happen is you have become a much wiser person. You need to remember in the end we only regret the chances we did not take!! So be enthusiastic about the purpose of your life. Don't be a goose!'

Two:
'A pessimist sees the difficulty in every opportunity, but an optimist sees the opportunity in every difficulty. You are what you think all day every day.

You have got to take responsibility for your own life and future.

We all like to create these big excuse lists as to why we are not doing well or successful, but the scary part is that we make excuses for our excuses to try and make ourselves look better. So pay attention to this as it's not what happens cos anything can happen, but what we do that makes a difference. So be a doer and don't be a goose!

Three:
'Today I want to talk to you about failure because people misunderstand failure. What I mean by this is that just because you fail does not make you a failure because all it creates is the ultimate stepping stone to greatness and success. All the greatest people in the

world have failed, but the key ingredient is not to give up and let persistence prevail. Once you understand this mindset you can achieve anything, so don't be a goose..!

Four:
Today I want to talk to you about imagination and how nothing in the world can be possible without it. All it takes in life is one idea and the persistence to achieve that idea to make it a reality. You see a builder does not just build an amazing building it takes an architects imagination and dream to construct such a piece of work, and this applies to absolutely everything in life, as someone had to use their imagination to create an idea for us to be able to use that product or service. So understanding the power of imagination open ups opportunity to make dreams a reality. So use your own power and don't be a goose..!'

Five:
'Today I want to talk about the future because we have lived in the past and we are clever enough we will have learned from our mistakes and will now be connecting the dots for your future as this is where we are going! There has to be purpose in everyone's life and to create purpose you have to have a destination and to have a destination you have to have a plan! Your future is what you make it, and only you get to choose what your future is but the big win here is understanding that only you can sabotage

your future and goals as excuses are for the weak! Be strong look to the future and don't be a goose!'

Six:

'Today I would like to talk to you about insanity! Insanity in my view is when people do the same things every day, week, month and year, year after year but for some reason expect things to get better in life! How is this even possible? The fact of the matter is, it is not unless you change something. You need to start stepping out of your comfort zone and start realising you have to work hard on yourself for change to happen. So are you willing to do things differently or are you going to just keep moaning that life is too difficult? Be courageous and don't be a goose!'

Seven:

'Today I want to talk to you about risks because you have to take risks to move forward in life but those risks are just challenges and hurdles you need to get over. When you were a baby, and you were learning to walk did you just quit and sit on your arse all day? No, when you fell down you got your arse back up and tried again and again and again until you were causing havoc running around everywhere and discovering new things. So that's all it takes a risk, a leap of faith and practice then you will start to find out what else you can achieve. So break the mould take a risk and don't be a goose!'

Eight:
'Today I want to talk to you about direction. Too many people have a lack of direction and are too quick to use excuses as to why they are going nowhere in life. This all comes down to having specific goals in your life because saying you don't have time is rubbish because everybody has 24 hours a day 7 days a week 52 weeks a year so be specific with your goals and your direction becomes clear don't be a goose!'

Nine:
'Today I'm going to talk to you about being relentless. You see you have greatness inside of you but to let the greatness shine through you have to be relentless, it does not matter how many times someone says no or how many times you fail because that's what relentless is! You have to refuse to be denied; you can't score a goal if you don't shoot so keep shooting and realise how many goals you can score! Become the best you can! Be relentless. Don't be a goose!'

Ten:
'Today I want to ask you if you're scared. Because if you have an idea or a dream and it doesn't scare you, and it doesn't take you out of your comfort zone then it's pointless! It's not a big enough vision. Because being scared of doing something different means, you are pushing your boundaries, you're believing in

the greatness that you have about yourself and realising you can do this! Don't be a goose!'

Eleven:
'Today I want to talk to you about possibility blindness! This is only an illness to people who don't want to work for their dreams and future; this is when you're not willing to open your mind and better yourself and develop yourself to realise what doors you are able to open with just a little passion and desire. You need to realise anything is possible if you're willing to put in the effort and stop complaining. Don't be blind to possibilities and don't be a goose!'

Twelve:
'Today I would like to talk you about pretending! So many people in life are pretending they have a dream or a goal in life when actually they have no intention of doing anything. Anyone can say they are going change a bad habit or Stop pretending to be someone or do something and commit yourself to your goals in life, be that person #GazzaBounce you have control over everything you do so kick out your subconscious, stop saying but and make the change. Don't be a goose!'

Thirteen:
'Today I want to ask you how do you see yourself? Because life can only get better when you work on yourself when you work on yourself everything you

desire in life then follows. It does not matter what others think of you but only what you think of yourself. You have to do exactly what's best for you, so make that decision, figure out what YOU want and pursue it passionately! Don't be a goose!'

Fourteen:
'Today I would like to ask you to never underestimate the power of DESIRE. You see DESIRE is a weapon we all possess if we are willing to set it free. If you truly believe to not bow to failure DESIRE will carry you to your dreams. All achievements in life must start with a burning DESIRE, and you must realise there is no such word as impossible! Don't be a goose!'

Fifteen:
'Today I would like to talk to you about having a positive attitude. A positive attitude is believing in everything you want to achieve; it's when you wake up in the morning knowing you're going to have a great day. Once you realise a positive attitude is all about you on the inside, you then realise how great you are. As Earl Nightingale said, you become what you think about all day long. So be positive and don't be a goose!'

Sixteen:
'Today I would like to talk to you about investing! Now when I say investing, I mean investing in you! Too many people know too much other people and

not enough about themselves. In this day and age, we are in a perfect situation to build a better self! Taking the time to look out for ourselves and invest in ourselves is the only way to make a better future. There are no excuses for not expanding our knowledge except for laziness invest in yourself and don't be a goose!'

Seventeen:
'Today I want to talk to you about choosing your future! Not only is it possible to choose your future but its necessary. It's necessary that you work on yourself and make your own decisions. I'm telling you your dreams are possible if you are willing to stretch yourself and challenge yourself. So go out there today, be courageous, believe in yourself and choose your own future. Don't be a goose!'

Eighteen:
'Today I would like to talk to you about priorities! Because if you want to make something of your life, if you want the success you have always craved then you need to get your priorities right! You need to prioritise what's most important to you to succeed. So this is the realisation that sacrifices need to be made! So the minute you realise that you are the priority, all direction becomes clear on the changes that are required of YOU. Get your priorities straight and don't be a goose!'

Nineteen:

'Today I want to talk to you about giving up. Too many people in life give up because they have a setback or they were told NO ONCE OR TWICE. Too many people give up because there friends and family tell them it's not possible! So let me tell you this! NEVER GIVE UP BECAUSE SOMEONE TOLD YOU, YOU CANT! At any given moment in time, you have the power to say, this is not how the story ends! Never give up and don't be a goose!'

Twenty:

'Today I want to talk about BEING GREAT AT SOMETHING! Too many people look at athletes and SUCCESSFUL people and think it's impossible to be like that! This is where you need to realise that all it takes is stepping out of your comfort zone and start committing yourself to who you want to be! You need to pour your heart and soul into becoming the real you that is dying to break through! It's only laziness that stops you from being great. So don't fear hard work and become great at something. Don't be a goose!'

Twenty-one:

'Today I want to talk about choices! You need to be making your own decisive conscious choices in life if you want a better future! If you don't like your job CHANGE IT. If you don't like your lifestyle CHANGE IT. If you don't like your diet CHANGE IT. If you don't like where your living CHANGE IT!

You see if you don't make the right choices all you're doing is creating excuses for not making your life better. Stop living the life you don't want and start choosing your own future. Make your own business CHOICES and don't be a goose!'

Twenty-two:
'Today I want to talk to you about MINDSET. You see MINDSET is the key to everybody's future and if you want a better future you need to progress. And progression is impossible without change, and if you can't change your mind, you cannot change anything. Having the right MINDSET stops bad habits and helps you focus on what you need to follow through on your dreams and create an awesome future! So start building your dreams today, create your MINDSET and don't be a goose!'

Twenty-three:
'Today I want to ask you to LET GO!! You see you must be willing to LET GO of who you have been, to become who you are meant to be! The possibility of having a dream come true is what makes life interesting and makes life worth living! So LET GO of the past and use your imagination to choose your own future. Believe in yourself, realise who YOU are meant to be, LET GO of who you have been and don't be a goose!'

Twenty-four:
'Today I want to talk to you about your LIMITS. Too many people put LIMITS on what they can achieve whether it be physical or your dreams. Well, I'm here to confirm that there are no LIMITS to what you can achieve out of life only plateaus and you must not stay there, you must break through your LIMITATIONS, go above and beyond these LIMITS to realise your true self! Embrace the difficulties that you face, push yourself through the LIMITS and don't be a goose!'

Twenty-five:
'Today I would like to talk about FEAR. You see if you want anything from life you have to face your FEARS head on. So you need to stop being afraid of what could go wrong and think of what could go right. FEAR is always going to be an obstacle we face to achieve what we want out of life but remember if your dreams don't scare you, they are not big enough dreams in the 1st place! So start reminding yourself every day FEAR is a good thing, you just need to learn not to be afraid of it FACE YOUR FEARS and don't be a goose!'

Twenty-six:
'Today I want to talk to you about CHARACTER because a person's CHARACTER should not be judged by how successful they are but by the setbacks they suffered when their backs are against the wall. No matter how great the setback, no matter

how great the failure or the fall, you just pick yourself back up brush yourself down and keep pushing forward and overcome whatever is in front of you! Now that is Character, that's true success. So let your true CHARACTER shine through and don't be a goose!'

Twenty-seven:
'Today I want to talk about how every single human being on this earth is the same because no matter who you are or where you are, we all suffer heartbreak and disappointments in life! So this is how mental attitude separates the laziest from the greats. Because if you have the right mental attitude, you know that a disappointment is just a minor setback on your road to accomplishing your dreams! So it's time to get rid of the stinking thinking, make sure you have the right mental attitude and don't be a goose!'

Twenty-eight:
'Today I want to talk to you about TIME; you see TIME is our most valuable asset because we have a timeline to achieve our dreams. The one thing you can't do is replace TIME, you cannot buy TIME, you cannot grow TIME, so the only thing you can do is lose TIME. So all this does is let us abuse how much TIME we actually have which leads to us getting too comfortable with ourselves and not realising this until it is too late. This is where you need the mind shift to understand how valuable TIME is because

you seriously need to stop killing TIME before TIME starts killing you. So stop damaging your lifespan and regretting you had more TIME to achieve your dreams and don't be a goose!'

Twenty-nine:
'Today I want to talk to you about FUELLING YOUR MIND. The way I look at this is the same as filling up your car! The more petrol or diesel you put in the further, you will always go! So ask yourself this? How far do you want to go and how big are your dreams? Because if you want to make something of yourself, you need to be learning, studying and training hard to achieve your dreams and the only way to do this is to FUEL YOUR MIND. How much time do you spend working on YOU?? So listen to audio books, read influential books and study whatever it takes to put you in a stronger position to be closer to what you deserve! So like I always say, you can be whatever you want to be if you just FUEL YOUR MIND and don't be a goose!'

Thirty:
'Today I want to talk to you about thinking big! When I talk about thinking big, I want you to know you're allowed!! Yes, you're allowed. We get held back by too many people telling us that can never happen to us! 99% of people in the world are convinced they are incapable of achieving great things and aim for mediocre and live mediocre lives!

Be part of the 1% and think big and forget all the reasons it won't work and believe in the one reason that will work! You are what you think all day every day, so think big and don't be a goose!'

Thirty-one:
'Today I want to talk to you about FOCUS. You see when someone tells you something can't be done, it's more a reflection of their limitations, not yours! What you need to understand is that your FOCUS determines your reality. I wake up every single morning truly believing today is going to be better than yesterday because I have my dreams and goals to FOCUS on and look forward to. So it's time for you to FOCUS on what matters in your life and let go of what doesn't and don't be a goose!'

Thirty-two:
'This morning I want you to make a decision, I want you to decide consciously what your purpose in life is? So what is guiding you? What is directing your focus? Is it the love for your family, is it fear, and is your past? Is it a desire to be someone greater than you are? You need to decide, but it only has to be something simple something you can live every single day! The most important thing is what is the purpose of your life? Whatever you want to do, do it now as there are only so many tomorrows! Make a decision and don't be a goose!'

Thirty-three:
'Today I want to talk to you about PAIN. Because something I have seriously learned over the years and that is that PAIN IS TEMPORARY. It may last for a minute, an hour, a day or maybe even a year but eventually if you believe in yourself it will subside and be removed from your life! But let me tell you this if you quit, if you give up on your dreams, PAIN WILL STAY WITH YOU FOREVER. So don't let PAIN be your enemy, let it be your driver to who you want to be in life. Remember NO PAIN NO GAIN and don't be a goose!'

Thirty-four:
'Today I want to talk about being over cautious. Too many people in life won't have much because they are to cautions! This is called the timid approach to life. You see this is why you have to take risks. Your here people say but what if this happens and if that happens what about this? So I better not try! Well if you don't try you will never know, will you! Life is a risk, investing your money is risky, starting up a business is risky, getting married is risky, having a baby is risky! It's all risky. The one guarantee is no matter what you're not going to make it out alive, and that's a fact. Just give it a go! What have you got to lose?? So don't live a timid life, don't be over cautious and don't be a goose!'

Thirty-five:
'Make it happen! Just make it happen! Don't let your dreams be dreams, yesterday you said tomorrow, so stop using the excuses and make it happen! Make your dreams come true! Just get on with it. While there are people in the land of nod dreaming of success, you're going to get up off your arse and do something about it; you're going to work hard at it, nothing is impossible!! If others want to quit that's fine but you are not going to quit, you're going to make it happen! What are you waiting for just make it happen! I believe in you so believe in yourself! If you're tired of starting over, then stop giving up make it happen and don't be a goose!'

Thirty-six:
'Today I want to talk about taking responsibility because you need to know it is your fault! Stop blaming your circumstances knowing you have the power to change them. Most people don't have the willingness to break bad habits and excuses become their lives! Be responsible for your own actions. Yes, life is hard but if you do the hard work now then life becomes easier later on, so take action now, be responsible because you have the responsibility for making your own dreams a reality! Stop being a blamer of others and the world and don't be a goose!'

Thirty-seven:
'Today I want to talk to you about Average. I just don't understand why anyone would just want to be

Average? I looked up the meaning of Average in the dictionary, and it says ordinary, typical, mediocre! Do you really want to be that person? The word even goes back to the 15th century and has a meaning of damaged goods! This is why you need to get yourself out of the mind-set of being Average and settling for that lifestyle. Think about it logically what would you rather see? An average film or an exceptional one? An average sports match of some kind or a thrilling exceptional, exciting one? Makes sense now doesn't it? Don't get sucked into accepting the norm life when you can do something about it. Make yourself valuable and set yourself apart from the average crowd! Be thrilling, be entertaining, be exceptional and don't be a goose!'

Thirty-eight:
'Surrounding yourself with why I call "Like Minded People" can only benefit how your future will unfold. It's so important who you hang around with in life as positive surroundings push you hard and make you want to succeed. Like-minded people push you and understand what and why you want to do things and only show encouragement towards you. When this happens, you get made accountable for your actions, and it just puts the biggest smile on your face. When you are surrounded by great people, you start to attract so much more greatness in life so start being choosy in who you hang around with, and you will feel the benefits and realise your dreams. Be a winner and don't be a goose!'

Thirty-nine:

'After watching *Match of the Day* on Sunday morning and listening to every single manager that won or got a result they were looking for, all you heard coming from them was: the passion that comes from my players, the focus, the determination to win, the organisation, the discipline! The positive words were endless that all sum up success. I know it's just an analogy, but that's all I talk about, and it shows you that no matter what you need these qualities and attributes to succeed in life! Being one step ahead of your opposition and having a fighting spirit has its rewards, so it's time to get your game face on and don't be a goose!'

Forty:

'It's GazzaBounce time and your daily dose of positive attitude. I want to tell you it's time to expose yourself to all the greatness that it's out there! I have just finished a great book by an amazing man Nigel Botterill's. The reason this book is so powerful to me is because I know 1st hand how passionate this man is about helping others succeed in life! His book is there to motivate and inspire people, and that's what it has done for me! So when I get home from my holiday I'm all over it and will start exposing myself to the abundance of information there is from inspiring amazing people to help push myself and challenge myself to be even better than what I am now so I can achieve the goals and dreams I have set myself. So expose yourself to all the greatness that is available and don't be a goose!'

Forty-one:
'I have just watched a film called *The Internship* for probably the 10th time! The reason for this is because it is so amazingly inspirational. Yes, it's a comedy, but the true meaning behind the film blows my mind! You have two guys down on their luck and no jobs and no future! So they decide to do something about that! And only their self-belief kept them going in a world that was so alien to them it was untrue. They decided to get the courage and step outside their comfort zones and just go for it and take that risk! So it just shows you it does not matter who you are or what stage in your life you are at! Yes it's scary, and yes you're allowed to be afraid, but if you're willing to be courageous, work hard and believe in yourself you can follow whatever dream you want and don't be a goose! So my question for you today is what films have you watched that truly inspire you and make you want to have a better future for yourself?'

Forty-two:
'Motivation is such a key element to having a positive attitude and an amazing start to any day! So today's positive quote is: some people often say motivation does not last, well neither does bathing that's why we recommend it daily. Being able to self-motivate yourself opens up all sorts of doors and

opportunities so find something that makes you jump out of bed ready for an amazing day and don't be a goose!'

Forty-three:
Your daily dose of positive attitude. Today I want you to be more wasp! Now I know they are annoying buggers, but they are persistent and know what they want! They keep coming back at you because they want that sticky item on your dinner table, no matter how many times you swat them and say no, they keep coming back at you saying I want it!! So I want you to do the same, I want you to keep following your goals and dreams and pursue them until you get them! Don't let anyone tell you no or you can't do that, it's your dream so don't give up! So be more wasp and don't be a goose!'

Forty-four:
'Inspiring other people is what is really making me push forward and keep on making these videos for you amazing people. Having a potential new client tell me that I have helped him get more focused and inspired just is such an amazing feeling for myself. Self-satisfaction from giving something back is the greatest. This is someone who is already successful but now needed a new goal in life, so it does not matter who you are or what you have achieved, you will always need goals in your life to help you move forward in the right direction. So set goals dream big and don't be a goose!'

Forty-five:
It's GazzaBounce time and your daily dose of
Positive Attitude.
It will hurt
It will take time
It will require dedication
It will require willpower
You will need to make some serious healthy decisive
decisions
It will require motivation
It will require self-discipline
It will require sacrifices
You will need to push your body and your mind to
the max
There will be temptation
But I promise you right here right now, once you
reach your goal, it will be so worth it.
So today is the day you start dreaming, set your goals
and don't be a goose!'

Forty-six:
'I got asked why I'm so happy the other day so I
thought I would share my answer with you all. The
reason I'm so happy is because I made a decision to
change my mind. People underestimate the power of
a changed mind. You can change your hair, you can
change your facial hair, and you can change your
clothes. You can change as much as you want on the
outside but if you don't change your mind nothing
else in your life will change. It will just keep
repeating the same routines day after day after day!

So it's time for you to make that decision today and change your mind so that you can achieve your dreams. Be happy and don't be a goose!'

Forty-seven:
'Today I want to talk about having a vision and being patient. I sat down and watched the Anthony Joshua fight, and this man is just a machine he is amazing. This has all come about from self-development, taking his time, being patient and setting goals to reach his ultimate dream. All the fighters he dispatches are just obstacles in the way, and he fears no one and believes in himself! He wants to fulfil his dream by winning the belts that will be the stepping stones to the heavyweight championship of the world! So look at this man from Watford achieving his dreams but to achieve your dream, you must 1st have one to follow! So don't be scared to dream big and start throwing them big punches of your own and you will get your own Personal Knockout! And I'm here to prove that there is more greatness to come out of Watford and from every other person in the world that dares to dream big! So it's time to be a champion and don't be a goose!'

Forty-eight:
'It's GazzaBounce time and your daily dose of positive attitude. Today I want to talk about pain because too many people suffer the same sort of pain all because of their current situation in life! People think because of where they are now, that's how their

life and future needs to be and you could not be so wrong, and I'm living proof of that along with so many others. This is where you need to sacrifice who you to become who you want to be. Growth is painful, change is painful, but there is nothing more painful than being stuck somewhere you don't belong! So stop living a life of pain, start creating the change and don't be a goose!'

Forty-nine:
'Today I want to talk about an amazing man that I met over the weekend and that man was Billy Schwer! This man truly blew my mind; he was an inspiration after listening to his story because he stood for exactly what I try to tell so many people. We are talking about a man who had a dream and worked his arse off night and day to achieve that dream! It was not easy, and it was going to take passion, desire and true commitment to reach that dream. Another thing Billy understood and that was that Failure was not the end it was just a stage to make him stronger on, and that's exactly what it did! Billy did not win his world title fight at the 1st attempt neither did he win on the 2nd or the 3rd but he had so much self-belief in himself and his ability he went back stronger and achieved his dream at the fourth attempt and became the light welter weight champion of the world. So my point here is anything is possible if you dare have a dream and have the balls to take consistent action in achieving it! Once you understand failure, you receive success in

abundance so to my man Billy, be more Schwer and don't be a goose!'

Fifty:
'Well I have had such an amazing week surrounding myself with so many inspirational people and today's shout out goes to my good friend Aaron Philips of FitStart. This man has been a massive part of my journey as well as so many others, but the thing that gets me the most is what Aaron has created and what he also stands for. This man had a dream, and that dream was to help others achieve their own dreams. He put on an awards ceremony for all of his clients but what he created was truly inspirational as he had a room full of people with so much love for him but more importantly so much love for one another because they were all achieving their own goals and dreams. This was because of one man that told them and showed them it was possible! So I wanted to share this to show you what one man can do if you dare have a dream and take consistent action in making shit happen! So Aaron keep being you and inspiring so many others to follow their own dreams and don't be a goose!'

Fifty-one:
'Stop waiting for opportunities and start creating them. I mean what are you waiting for? Are you just going to sit and hope your lottery numbers come in for the rest of your life? No, you're not because you know that idea in your head, that restlessness that is

always telling you that you deserve better, well it's time to start paying attention and that time starts right here, right now! Opportunities are created through persistence and visualisation. So it's time to bounce out of that warm comfy bed in the mornings and stop letting opportunities pass you by! You are what you think about so stop waiting and start believing, start achieving and don't be a goose!'

Fifty-two:
'Today I want you to close your eyes and imagine the best possible version of you! That's who you really are, so you need to let go of any part of you that does not believe it. The 1st step of getting what you want is having the courage to get rid of what you don't. You see you have 2 choices in the mornings. Continue to sleep with your dreams or wake up and chase them! So when you close your eyes, that version of you is the dream, so chase the vision and don't be a goose!'

Fifty-three:
'It's GazzaBounce time and your daily dose of positive attitude and this morning I want to give you a brief description of what FEAR actually stands for. So FEAR has two meanings, the 1st is Forget everything and run and the second is Face everything and rise. So what does FEAR stand for in your life? Because the choice is only yours to make! So take this with you today you amazing people: Life is not about finding yourself, Life is about creating

yourself! So make today the day that YOU face everything and rise and don't be a goose!'

Fifty-four:

'Today I want to ask you what your pitch is. When you wake up every single morning what are you pitching to yourself and what are your expectations? There are two types of pitch, the first being: I can't believe I have to get up and go to work, I'm going to have a rubbish day, and I'm never going to be able to get enough money to go on holiday! Or you have the positive, enthusiastic pitch where you know today is going to be awesome because you truly believe that no matter what happens today it's going to get you 1 step closer to your dreams and goals! Pitching to yourself is empowering because whichever one you choose it will shape and decide your future, so if I believe in you its time you started believing in yourself! So make sure your pitch has plenty of bounce and don't be a goose!'

Fifty-five:

'Gazza Bounce time and your daily dose of positive attitude. So I want to ask you this morning? Do you wake up with determination and go to bed with satisfaction every single day? Because making small daily improvements are key to staggering long-term results! Motivation comes from looking at the things you want and realising what it takes to get it! So how about this for a powerful thought to take into the day!

So change your mind, change your attitude, change your situation and don't be a goose!'

Fifty-six:
'Inner motivation and inspiration have been key elements in getting me to where I am today! I wanted to share my story because I think it is relevant for you all to know that I do practice what I preach. Everything I talk about I take action on and implement to the best of my abilities. It's also important that you understand that it's not all been sunshine and roses, but it's making sure you get past the naysayers in your life and surround yourself with the right influential people who will help you reach your goals and want to help you on your journey. My story is being shared as I want to inspire others to believe in themselves and truly understand that if you're willing to make sacrifices and work hard now, life does get easier! So please, please follow your heart and your dreams and don't be a goose!'

Fifty-seven:
'The reason so many people in the world resist change is because they focus far too much on what they have to give up instead of the real focus of what there is to actually gain! Sacrifice is part of any true journey. You need to understand that plans are useless because the real power is in the actual planning!! It's time to start prioritising your life otherwise without hesitation the world and others will do it for you! Clarity is key, Clarity is necessary,

Clarity is absolute so to focus on the gain you need to commit and don't be a goose!'

Fifty-eight:
'It's Gazza Bounce time and your daily dose of positive attitude. Now, this is something I wanted to touch on this morning because what do you think a positive attitude is? Because to me a positive attitude does not mean that things might turn out ok, a positive attitude is knowing that YOU will be ok no matter how things turn out! A positive attitude gives you power over your circumstances, instead of your circumstances having power over you! What you need to remember is that your attitude determines your direction, attitude is everything! It's a new day, its new strengths, its new thoughts so think positive, be positive and positive things will happen and don't be a goose!'

Fifty-nine:
'What are you reading this morning? What are you reading every day? Because if you are not learning, you are not earning! Make the most of your time by increasing your knowledge and developing your future! So remember if you are not willing to learn, no one can help you. But if you are determined to learn, no one can stop you! Don't allow the world to define your greatness because your power will always be unlimited. Education and knowledge is a power that can change the world, so why not change yours? And don't be a goose!'

Sixty:

'It's GazzaBounce Time and your daily dose of positive attitude and today I just want to talk about not missing out on the things you love. We all work so hard we sometimes let the important things pass us by that we regret later in life. So it is important that you recognise what's most important to you! One of the most important things for me is making sure that me and Keane get to go to as many Manchester United games as we can spending that father-son quality time together! And I have made sure I have taken the right action on getting my business and family life balance right so that I can do the things that are most important to me! Get your priorities right, and your world falls into alignment and don't be a goose!'

Sixty-one:

'It's GazzaBounce time and your daily dose of positive attitude. So this morning I actually quite excited as I have one my wonderful analogies for you to share. You I had the whole day off yesterday because it's half term and I wanted to spend the day with my youngest Keane, and we went to watch PAN. Now, this got my mind working overtime and just thought Peter Pan is just like real like if you look at it properly. Let's take the main parts for example and use it as part of my life. So we Captain Hook, he is our biggest fear. Then we have the Pirates; they are our obstacles. Then the lost boys, my family, friends and staff. Then Peter Pan, me the boy who never grows old!! Now we all know peter pans biggest strength is happy thoughts, being positive, self-belief and with this strength, he can then fly and fight. So you are flying your lost boys now believe in you they want to follow you, they want to support you. So now you have unity, and you can face and fight those pirates and push them out of the way. Then you come face to face with Captain Hook, but you believe in yourself so much, and you have your lost boys behind you, so you stand tall and defeat him and feed him to that big bad crocodile. So do you see where I'm coming from? We all have a Peter Pan inside of us, and we have to stop thinking of all the crap and bad things we have done and just focus on our happy thoughts, believe in yourselves and face our fears head on! Everyone needs to have something to aim for so make sure you are following your dreams because Neverland is out there if you want it bad enough! So be Peter Pan and don't be a goose!'

Sixty-two:
'It's Gazza Bounce time and your daily dose of positive attitude, and I really want to talk about upgrades and updates. Because we are so conscious in this day and age about technology and making sure with, have the latest upgrade on our phones, TV and computers. Also, we always are waiting for the latest software update to make our product even better and even faster the one thing we forget to do is Upgrade and update our own personal software! We need to start focusing on what is most important and

that is enhancing ourselves, enhancing and increasing our knowledge base. When you are learning, you are increasing your skill set and getting the opportunity to decide and create your own future. Upgrade yourself, do your daily updates and don't be a goose!'

Sixty-three:
'It's GazzaBounce time and your daily dose of positive attitude. One of the most successful things for me throughout my life and my journey so far is not being arrogant about knowing! But to embrace the fact that I have a weakness, we all have a weakness, and that is not knowing a lot about something! Not being arrogant and realising that I need to learn more about the things I don't know keeps me striving forward and making my life better. Never be afraid of not knowing because someone will always be able to guide you, there will always be a book you can read on the subject. Not knowing gives you the ability to learn and with learning comes knowledge. But knowledge useless without action. Never be afraid of not knowing. If you're not learning, you're not earning. So grab knowledge with both hands and conquer your weakness just like I did and don't be a goose!'

Sixty-four:
'It's GazzaBounce time and your daily dose of positive attitude. My video is about the two most important steps to success and achieving your

dreams. Because you have to have a vision and a dream if you want the best things in life for you and your family. So the first step is ambition! You have to want the success so bad that you're willing to run through walls to achieve it! And the second step is Action, taking action means that you are creating and when you are creating you are making a positive change to your life. So the question is, do you have what is needed to make these two steps to success? With these two steps there are two options, make progress or make excuses so believe in yourself and don't be a goose!'

Sixty-five:
Its GazzaBounce time and your daily dose of positive attitude this morning my video has two parts, and I want to talk about no pain, no gain. As a lot of you know, I was up for a bounce-back award yesterday which I did not win, but I have to say my story felt like a little dot compared to some of the pain that the other finalists have been through! Don't get me wrong your own dot is always massive when it's your own but the true strength I saw in others yesterday inspired me like you could not believe! They turned their pain into their biggest gain because they had so much self-belief. We have to understand that pain is a part of life and it's something embrace because it's not going to go away! So I salute all you amazing people for showing that true determination and fighting spirit to bounce back and show that there is no gain without pain. Also big congratulations to

every award winner yesterday because for how successful each and every one of them is I'm sure they can back up the pain they have gone through to become the success that they are.

Part two of my video is that I did it, I have gone white, and it hurt! The pain I went through for five hours to make this happen was immense but whatever pain went through is only Ossie's and rays of sunshine's gain! So remember pain will always be a part of life no matter which way you turn but it's up to you to believe in yourself enough to learn from it and make it your ultimate gain. So keep being amazing and don't be a goose!'

Sixty-six:
Its Gazza Bounce time and your daily dose of positive attitude and this morning I want to talk to you about foundations. You are you laying the right foundations for your life? The reason I ask this is because I watched the Vidal Sassoon documentary and his story blew my mind. You have a man who spent his childhood in an orphanage and got a job as an apprentice hairdresser by chance. But he put his heart and soul into becoming the best because he studied and trained so hard and he knew what was needed to become the best! He even realised that his cockney accent was not going to take him to the top as people would not take him serious enough, so he took elocution lessons to improve his communication skills. But for all of his success for the first nine years, he said true success was when he created the

five-point haircut, and that was what all the foundations and hard work were for! That haircut changed his life for the better. You see too many people are looking for quick-fix success when it's not out there, true success only come from a desire and repetitive, consistent hard work, and this is done by laying your foundations and educating yourself in the right areas! Vidal Sassoon said that the only time success comes before work is in the dictionary! So make sure you are building your future now by laying the right foundations and don't be a goose!'

Epilogue

To finish a book, it is important to have an impact and this final part I hope will inspire you every day. Feel free to rip it out and pin on your fridge door or office wall or copy it and pass it around. When you read this, I recommend you read it aloud and you will feel the passion, and it will start your day in a positive way. Thanks for staying until the end. And remember, don't be a goose!

I Vow To Succeed

When it comes to achieving my dreams there is no point in being concerned about failing; it is more important to believe in the power of getting up.

Every time I fall or fail, I promise to bounce back and return for more. It is vital to keep on returning to make my dreams come true. Giving up or giving in isn't an option. Like a true warrior, I know the battle will be long and hard, but I also know I have the strength and capabilities to succeed. Even if others don't believe in me or what I can do, I believe I can, and my vision ensures that I can achieve all the things I set out to do.

No one has the power, ability or right to define what I can and cannot do and the doubts of others are my motivation to keep powering on. It doesn't matter how many people try to prevent me from achieving my dreams, they cannot block me, and I will never give up.

There will be times when pain is present, but pain can be a powerful ally, pushing me onto bigger achievements and success. Pain helps you to develop a stronger version of yourself, and this is why I welcome pain and thrive on working with it.

I believe that pain is part of the journey and I am thankful for the chances I have been provided with, earned and taken. While I am proud of how far I have come, I will always strive to achieve more, and I aim to achieve all of my dreams. This is what I have worked for and what I am working towards.

Every passing second, minute, hour and day is an opportunity to move forward and improve my life, and even though there are obstacles, I do not fear them. In going through such things you create a clearer path, developing an even clearer vision of where you are going and what you are looking to achieve.

I am not a finished product, I am working hard to improve every day, and one simple goal in life is to be better today than what I was yesterday. Everyone in the world should be looking to improve each day, and I am not the only person with these desires and this outlook.

This is the ideal time, this is the moment, and I promise to do everything in my power to ensure that I make myself a better person every day. This cannot be achieved without hard work and dedication. I respect the level of effort required, and I vow to succeed in my journey.

(Editor's note: this section was originally in the body of the book, but as publishers, we felt this was the perfect way to end such a positive book. We hope you agree.)

You can follow, and contact, Gary using these links:

www.dontbeagoose.co.uk

www.gooseclothing.co.uk

gary@dontbeagoose.co.uk

facebook.com/dontbeagoose

He is also on YouTube as Gary Fullwood – look him up and subscribe to his regular doses of positivity on video.

Ossie – 'The Bravest Boy I Know'

The reason I am standing here today is to have an opportunity to share the effect Ossie had on my life and to say thank you.

When you are lucky enough to have had an Ossie in your life like all of us here today, you realise the true power of togetherness, of love, strength and courage.

Ossie simply had everything in his locker and knew what he wanted and exactly how to get it too. He had charm, charisma, determination, passion, affection and love. Let's not forget his everlasting cheekiness as well. The list goes on for what Ossie brought to the world and the impact he had. Without him being a part of this world and my life I may not have had the courage to face my own fears, the challenges and obstacles, to keep fighting what I truly believe in.

Ossie made me understand what never giving up meant and I know full well that no matter what journey I want to take or path I decide to pursue, Ossie will always be by my side urging me to follow my heart and my dreams.

Ossie has affected, and touched, the hearts and lives of so many people in so many different ways. He will be smiling right now and looking down on us all knowing he has left his mark on the world.

Don't Be A Goose

I want you all to remember that no matter how hard you think the day is; in whatever you are doing or the challenges and obstacles that you may face. If you remember Ossie's smile and the amazing strength that came with it, then I can assure you, right here and now, you will be, and do, just fine.

Ossie, you are, and will always be my hero. My inspiration and my strength. I can promise you that your smile will always be with me and I will never give up; for as long as you are looking down on me.

'Ossie – the bravest boy I know.'

I will always love you, big man x

Don't Be A Goose